UNRAVELED

Support for *UNRAVELED*

"While the death of a child is every parent's worst nightmare, this book is filled with intelligent hope born from such a sacred pain. Kyle and Betty have taken their experience of deep loss, and with authenticity and resilience, they lay bare the devastation they have endured and the joy they have created. Theirs is a shared narrative of great beauty through profound suffering."
—**Dr. Melissa Mork**, Professor of Psychology and Grief Counselor

"In *Unraveled*, the Mertens share their tragic yet transformative journey, generously opening their hearts—and their personal journal—for others to learn from. It offers an authentic and inspiring look at how one couple extracted meaning, love, and life from the most unimaginable loss. And yet, the concepts in *Unraveled* are universal and broadly applicable as they suggest a hopeful way forward when suffering with grief and loss of any kind."
—**Julie Winkle Giulioni**, International Bestselling Author

"If I could only recommend one book for the rest of my days, it would be *Unraveled*. In a world of isolating narratives about "what's normal," it's far too easy to feel alone and wrong in our experience of grief. Kyle and Betty not only normalize loss, the revolutionary help they offer feels like a breath of long overdue fresh air. They dispel myths about grief and trauma that make us believe we should be "doing it better." They offer accessible, thoughtful guidance to find your own way forward. And by writing it with their two unique voices, they beautifully model what they propose: there's no one way to do this, and any way is easier with help. It's a down-to-earth yet inspiring invitation to open to your own humanity. More than help you "get through loss," this book will help you take yourself through it, one messy, raw, loving, supported step at a time."
—**Kirsten Parker**, Decision Coach

"This book beautifully wraps words around thoughts and feelings that are difficult to express."

—**Jenn and Mark Hinkle**, Founders of
The Ollie Hinkle Heart Foundation

"Ella's legacy touched our lives long before this book was written. After we lost our son Jackson, Kyle and Betty used their journal to help support us through a dark time when no one else knew what to say. *Unraveled* is an inspiring resource for anyone learning to live and love after loss."

—**Ben and Lara Gillham**, Co-Founders of
Just Enduring: Living and Loving After Child Loss

"Too often parents must face a reality that is dark and unbearable. They walk a path that feels lonely and filled with pain and despair. Betty and Kyle have walked this path, and now *Unraveled* is their gift to all who have experienced a similar loss, and the pain, guilt, and anger that accompany it. This book was written in the hopes it will light the paths of many others. But *Unraveled* goes beyond just its writing and wisdom. It sprang forth from empathy and compassion to yield heart-felt guidance and advice just when it's needed the most."

—**Dan Wright**, Owner of Fitting Words Publishing

"What a gift to enter into the honest, raw, and thoughtful journey of Betty and Kyle with the loss of their precious daughter. They mark the complexity of grief and loss while seeking wholeness and finding rays of goodness. This book is a blessing for those who may not understand the depth of grief and those who are walking through their own journey. Thank you, Betty and Kyle, for giving your heart to others through this book."

—**Dr. Amy Bragg-Carey**, President of Friends University

"*Unraveled* is the light that guides you through the dark tunnel of loss and tragedy."

—Jen Bastien, Cardiac ICU RN at
St. Louis Children's Hospital

"I cannot express how much I absolutely love this book. I started noting some of my favorite parts but stopped when I realized it was basically the entire book. The real-life examples are amazing, and I really appreciate how Kyle and Betty both provide their own unique perspectives and advice. The layout is great, and I like how it is set up so that it can be read in parts or all at once. I think *Unraveled* has the ability to help people feel less isolated in their grief, and I am looking forward to sharing it with others."

—**Allison Remy**, Licensed Clinical Social Worker

"Kyle and Betty give context to the chaos of having your world turned upside down by child loss. While their experience is unique, the emotions and struggles in the aftermath of child loss are similar to many other parents on this journey. We wish we would have had the honesty and advice in this book when our daughter Everly passed."

—**Nick and Martha McGeehon**, Co-Founders of
Just Enduring: Living and Loving After Child Loss

"I've seen so many families in my time as a physician who could have benefited from the personal and heartbreaking details Kyle and Betty candidly share in *Unraveled*. The impact Kyle and Betty have already made on pediatric congenital heart disease is inspiring, and *Unraveled* is the next step in their moving journey to help others."

—**Dr. Kory Lavine**, MD, PhD,
Washington University Cardiologist

UNRAVELED

When Loss
Changes Everything

KYLE AND BETTY MERTENS

KYLE AND BETTY BOOKS
St. Louis, Missouri

Unraveled: When Loss Changes Everything
Copyright © 2022 Kyle and Betty Mertens

Published by Kyle and Betty Books
St. Louis, Missouri

ISBN paperback: 979-8-9856533-0-4
ISBN ebook: 979-8-9856533-1-1

Library of Congress Control Number: 2022902693

Editorial Services: The Writer's Ally
Book Design: Clarity Designworks

www.kyleandbetty.com

Contents

In loving memory of Ella Marie Mertens,
who enriched our lives beyond imagination
April 4, 2016 — May 15, 2017

Foreword

Chances are if you're reading this book, you or someone you know is in the worst storm of their life. A life-changing, soul-shattering storm of impossible loss, trauma, and grief. A storm so big it seems like it will never end.

It's unfair.

It's cruel.

It literally sucks the oxygen from your lungs.

It is a storm no one wants, but so many of us endure. It's a storm my dear friends Betty and Kyle have been walking through since 2017 when they unexpectedly lost their beloved daughter Ella shortly after her first birthday. As much as we want to make these storms end, the truth is that storms like these never really end... but they don't rage with the same ferocity forever either. They change, and so do our hearts.

Our instinct when we, or those we love, are in pain, is to try and make the pain stop. But we can't make pain stop. Feelings don't work that way. They are called feelings because they need to be felt, not stopped, stifled, or ignored. Our human nature isn't comfortable with profound suffering. When we are face to face with our trauma, or another person's trauma, we are often paralyzed by our inability to fix it. When those we love are suffering, we want to make it better—both for them, and for ourselves—because to live in a world where impossible tragedy and pain can just exist terrifies us for our own security as well.

So, how do we do this? How do we keep breathing through our worst moments? How do we find meaning when we are shattered? How do we weave ourselves back together when we are unraveled? How do we come alongside those we love who are in immense pain? Words don't make it better and the absence of words makes it worse, so where do we go? What do we do?

We do it together.

We partner with people in their impossible moments, and we walk together.

Step by step.

Breath by breath.

We do it together.

The profound trauma of loss changes us. It changed me. The sudden loss of my father when I was ten and the subsequent abandonment by my mother nearly destroyed me. Thirty years later the pain still lives in me, but it doesn't consume me like it used to. Instead, it empowers me to come alongside others who are grieving with a profoundly empathetic heart. The ferocity of my pain has become a ferocity to love. Coming alongside those who have experienced similar loss is where healing begins. I was lost in the isolation of my grief for many years. I wish younger me had had allies like Betty and Kyle in her life so she wouldn't have been so alone in her suffering.

Our suffering unites us. We don't get to choose our suffering, but we do get to choose what we do with it. Betty and Kyle were unraveled by the loss of their precious Ella, but they have woven their experience into this incredible resource to help you navigate your grief. In this book they've taken their impossible and used it to partner with you, in the middle of your impossible, to make something new possible.

—Bree Smith-Friedrichs,
Personal Friend and Award-Winning Meteorologist

Dear Reader, Start Here

This book is not a memoir. It is less about us telling our story and more about connecting with others who have suffered loss. We aren't doctors or celebrities, but we have experienced a depth of grief that is unimaginable to most folks, and that grief has made us unlikely experts. Our goal is to walk along beside people in pain and provide encouragement. We don't claim to have all the answers, but we can share some insights we have learned on our journey so far.

One thing we can promise is that this book will not make your heart heavy. The last thing people need in sad moments is a heavy book. We will share pieces of our story to help provide context, but our focus will be less on the trauma of the past and more on how it has shaped our future.

You will see quickly that our personal experience involves the unexpected loss of our daughter Ella. Although our book is written based on our experience, the concepts are not exclusive to child loss. So many overarching themes are applicable to any situation involving loss. The loss doesn't even have to be a death. Sometimes there is grief associated with the loss of a relationship, or even just a plan you had for your life.

Unfortunately, grief is very messy. If you are looking for a clear, step-by-step guide, you won't find it in this book. The grieving process unravels differently for every person, and we would never sign up for trying to map it out. Instead, we will focus more on the big picture and provide insights for the overall journey.

Lastly, this book won't fix anything. Some things can't be fixed. What we have realized is that when we can't fix it, the next best thing is to figure out how to move forward with our new reality. In the pages that follow, that is what we are going to do. We are going to talk about what it looks like to live in this new world that is very different from anything we have chosen for ourselves. It is certainly tangled and complicated, but in the end, we have found that it is far from ruined.

Our Story

Our lives will not be ruined by this tragedy.

WHEN IT RAINS

Every happy couple dreams of the perfect wedding day filled with magic. Our special day was filled with something a little extra . . . rain. And it wasn't a cute little sprinkle here and there—it was a torrential downpour all day. You may have heard the saying that rain on your wedding day is good luck. I'm pretty sure someone just made that up in an effort to console a poor bride who was melting down while abandoning all hopes for beautiful outdoor photos.

I am happy to report that there were no meltdowns at the Mertens wedding, at least not on account of the rain. We quickly improvised and purchased a lifetime-worth of black umbrellas. We moved the location of the outdoor photos to a park with a variety of covered areas. It's a little funny that even though our wedding took place in downtown St. Louis, we didn't manage to get a single photo with the Arch in the background.

Despite all the complications caused by the rain, our wedding day was still magical. In fact, one of my favorite photos was taken in the middle of a downpour. We were holding an umbrella and laughing together under a covered area at the park. I obviously had no idea what the future had in store for us—no clue that that tender moment would be a metaphor for the unchangeable chaos we would encounter later in life.

As you are well aware, sometimes we are faced with circumstances outside of our control that just suck. If I could go back and change the weather on my wedding day, I would. I can't. It's not even a helpful exercise to waste my mental energy on it. Instead, I look back at those pictures and appreciate the imperfect beauty. We were dealt a hand that was less than ideal, but no amount of rain could steal our joy.

BEST-LAID PLANS
From the start of our relationship, Kyle and I always had a plan. Here is the basic outline:
1) Get married.
2) Finish our MBAs.
3) Take an exotic trip to celebrate.
4) Build our family home.
5) Have a baby.
6) Have a second baby about two years later.

Well, as you have probably guessed, that's not quite how things went down for us. We managed to get through steps one to five, but that's where everything went off the rails. Neither of us could have imagined how our story would unfold from there. Life has a way of throwing you some unexpected curveballs. Now here we are writing a book, which was never part of the plan.

The fact that you are even reading this book means it's likely you or someone you care about has experienced one of those curveballs. A significant change to the life you had envisioned for yourself can create a darkness that is very difficult to overcome. Sometimes seeing someone else who has faced a similar darkness and come out on the other side provides hope. Perhaps the best place to start is by sharing where all our plans went sideways.

OUR CURVEBALL

Warning: This section provides details about our daughter's death, which could be triggering. Feel free to skip ahead to the next section.

On April 4, 2016, we were overjoyed to welcome our beautiful daughter Ella into the world. In her first twelve months, Ella flourished, teaching us everything we needed to know about being first-time parents. She learned how to crawl and say her favorite words, "Dada" and "What's that?" She loved playing peekaboo, balancing on her daddy's hand, and pretending like she could read. Ella was also a little jet-setter, accompanying us on trips to Portland, Destin, Las Vegas, Minneapolis, Branson, and many other destinations. We were a happy little family.

In April 2017 Ella started showing signs of sickness. At first, she just seemed to have a cold. We took her to the hospital because we noticed she was wheezing, but we had no idea that her noisy breathing was a symptom of a much bigger problem. Not long after Easter, Ella was admitted to St. Louis Children's Hospital. She was in heart failure. This news came completely out of left field, especially because no history of heart disease existed in either of our families. The doctors thought it was brought on by a virus. After one tough week in the hospital, Ella's condition seemed to improve. She was released to come home. She still had obstacles to overcome, but everyone thought the worst was over. We had weekly check-ups following her release, and Ella seemed to be progressing well. The tests suggested her health was improving.

We woke up on May fifteenth, Kyle's thirtieth birthday, not imagining that it would be the day we would lose our daughter. We planned to leave for a tropical vacation the following day, so we were each tying up loose ends at work when we got the call from daycare that Ella's lips were turning blue. In a panic, we rushed to meet her in the ER where we were told that she would need to be transferred via helicopter to St. Louis Children's Hospital.

Knowing the helicopter had room for only one passenger, we decided Kyle would drive to the hospital. We figured he would arrive around the same time as the chopper, so he kissed Ella goodbye and left. Those would be his final moments with her.

As Ella and I waited for the chopper, she seemed so helpless and scared. I tried my best to comfort her, promising her she could have more of the Tater Tots she loved at Children's Hospital. I told her how brave she was and how I would take lots of pictures of her in the helicopter so she could show all her friends at daycare.

When the paramedics arrived with the chopper, they informed me that Ella's breathing tube needed to be adjusted. They said it would be uncomfortable for her and that the helicopter would be very loud, so they wanted to sedate her a little to keep her calm. I held her hand as her eyes closed and the EMTs started working on her breathing tube. It was then that she flatlined.

Chaos broke out as the medics worked to resuscitate her. I called Kyle via video on my phone so he could see what was happening. Even in those moments I fully expected them to bring her back. I handed my phone to a nurse so Kyle could continue to see what was going on while I moved to the head of her bed to sing her favorite song, "Que Sera Sera," over her.

I don't even remember when they stopped the compressions. It wasn't until everyone had stepped away from the bed that I stopped singing. My initial response was to try and wake myself up. I was certain that this was a nightmare, and if I could snap out of it, I would find Ella sleeping peacefully in her crib. Instead, reality crashed against me like a tidal wave as I stared at my husband's tormented face on my phone. There was no waking up from this. She was gone.

They let me hold her as I waited for Kyle to return. I just sat there, pushing my thumb into her little palm so I could feel her tiny fingers curl around it. I thought about all the plans we had envisioned for her, all the memories we would never get to make. I thought about how Kyle would never get to walk her down the aisle. I thought about how we would never get to see the beautiful woman she should have become.

Her death came as a complete shock to everyone, including the medical professionals. It wasn't until six weeks later that results from a genetic test revealed that Ella had a very rare heart mutation that led to dilated cardiomyopathy, which means her heart became too large to function effectively. After she passed, moving forward seemed overwhelming, but we were determined not to let this tragedy destroy us.

THE JOURNAL

In the months that followed Ella's death, Kyle and I wanted to be very intentional about communicating with each other. We had heard many stories of tragedies like ours unraveling relationships. In an effort to be proactive about sharing our thoughts and feelings with each other, we started a journal together. It wasn't anything fancy, just a moleskin notebook with unlined pages. We used it to keep track of our discussions so we could look back on them later. I kept it in my purse, and I would pull it out and add to it any time we had a meaningful conversation. The pages were filled with messy bullet points and often stained with tears and little splashes of wine. It was our unceremonious way of reflecting on all the concepts and stories that helped us as we worked through our grief.

What we didn't realize at the time was how handy that little journal would become. Something extraordinary happens when you go through tragedy. It uniquely qualifies you to support others. This phenomenon became clear to us when people started reaching out for insight on all types of painful situations—the loss of a loved one, a terminal diagnosis, a divorce, a child diagnosed with a genetic condition, and more. Frequently people wanted our advice on what to say or do to help a loved one who was suffering. They often asked questions about what we did to get through our grief. Sometimes they would even ask if they could put us in direct contact with someone who was grieving.

As we entered into these difficult conversations, we found ourselves constantly referencing our journal. We realized that the stories and thoughts that helped us through our most challenging times also seemed to resonate with others. Sometimes after those conversations, people would ask us if they could have a copy of our notes to look back on, but our journal was just a compilation of fragmented thoughts. It required context and explanation. We needed to find a more practical way to share it, which is what led us to write this book.

You are essentially holding our journal. The handwritten sections at the beginning of the chapters are direct quotes from its pages. Each chapter is told from one of our two perspectives, but all the content is reflective of conversations we had together. We have taken our messy notes, sorted them into similar concepts, provided context, and weaved them together in an effort to walk with you through whatever loss you are facing.

BEYOND WORDS

So, what do you say to someone when their world comes apart at the seams? No words are adequate. Grief is such a complex emotion, and everyone handles it differently. In fact, it can vary in the moment by individual. For example, one minute you may really want someone to ask you how you are doing so you can talk about it, and the next you might just want everyone to treat you like normal. There is no "right" approach.

To make matters worse, when people don't know what to say, they tend to just quietly observe. Unfortunately, enhanced scrutiny is about the last thing you need when you are dealing with overwhelming grief. During an emotionally vulnerable time, it can feel like you're living in a glass house. This is part of what made the journal such a helpful tool for us. It provided a safe space to process our grief without any judgment. We could write down all the raw thoughts or feelings we were having without filtering them. Somehow having them all on paper provided a sense of clarity.

One thing that surprised us looking back at our notes was how many of them were tied to stories from our past. It became very evident how each experience in our lives had unknowingly helped shape us for the journey ahead. Lessons we learned in seemingly mundane situations resurfaced in light of our tragedy to help us make sense of what we were experiencing.

Our hope is that by sharing our stories, we can encourage you to reflect on your own experiences. Nobody is ever prepared to deal with tragedy, but when we think back, we can find applicable lessons we've learned along the way to help. We can't offer any science for piecing it all together, so the best we can do is share what we found to be helpful. We encourage you to learn what you can from our stories and then build on them with lessons you've learned from your own experience.

If it is any comfort, what we have found in talking to other grieving people is that nobody has it totally figured out. We are all just learning as we go. Grief is not linear, so some days will be harder than others. The whole process takes more time than any of us want it to, and although the pain never fully goes away, it does get better. We aren't sure where you are on the journey, but take comfort in knowing you're not alone. We can't fix whatever it is you are dealing with, but we can certainly walk beside you for a while.

Part 1

Glimmers in the Dark
Getting Through the First Days

ENTERING THE TUNNEL

People often compare feelings of grief to ocean waves. At the beginning, the waves are relentless. It feels like you can't catch your breath before another one crashes into you, pulling you under. Over time the magnitude subsides and the waves become more spaced out, but on any given day, a rogue wave has the power to knock you off your feet. Eventually, you start to see them coming so you can brace yourself for impact.

Although we have found this analogy to be accurate, it's not incredibly helpful early on when you feel like you're drowning. In our experience, the beginning of grief felt very much like entering a huge, dark tunnel. A stark contrast existed between our life before and our life after losing Ella. The path in front of us seemed pitch black, but the memories of our daughter were still fresh, and the warm support of family and friends did cast some residual light.

We remember the day when we finally had to throw away all the flowers from the memorial. That was the first time we truly felt the darkness closing in on us. Everyone else was moving on with their lives, but nothing would ever be the same for us. We didn't want to move on. We just wanted to go back to the way things were. We felt completely trapped. Even though we knew that it wouldn't be like this forever, the darkness felt suffocating.

At that time, the light at the end of the tunnel didn't even seem appealing. We weren't ready to find our new normal, but we were getting farther from the light at the *mouth* of the tunnel. We just needed a flicker of hope to ward off the darkness. Reflecting on these next few stories is what helped us get through those initial months after the memorial. Although nothing could change the fact that our situation was ridiculously awful, these reflections felt like coming up for air in very heavy moments.

CHAPTER 2

Finding Beauty

I want to live in a way where I don't have regrets because I have thoroughly appreciated the things I have while I have them.

BEAUTY IN THE DUSTING

You know the type of person who is so busy that you can't imagine how they could possibly fit another thing on their plate? I fall into that category. I tend to fill my life so full that it constantly brims over the edges. I was no different back in high school. Between school, homework, extracurricular activities, friends, and other responsibilities, I was constantly on the move.

When I met a sweet woman who had cerebral palsy and was looking for someone to help clean her house once a week, I naturally offered my services. She was very capable and needed my assistance with only three basic tasks: dusting, window washing, and vacuuming. Even though I genuinely loved helping her, I had so many other obligations that by the time I arrived at her house every week, I was flying low.

I always began with the dusting, and I swore this woman had more knickknacks than any other person on the planet. Moving each little statue and figurine became the bane of my existence. I remember thinking every week, *If I could just get to the window washing, at least I wouldn't have to move anything. Or better yet, if I were vacuuming, I'd be almost finished.* But there I was, stuck in the doldrums of dusting, at the farthest point in my night from being able to head home.

Then, like some kind of lame reward for all the time spent fiddling with knickknacks, I was able to move on to the glorious task of window washing. I'm not sure if it was the strange off-brand cleaner or perhaps the coarse paper towels, but for some reason I was plagued by streakiness. I painstakingly worked toward a sparkling surface only to leave a giant streak with my last swipe (insert head bang into said mirror or window). In the moment, I longed for the dusting, remembering how simple it was when I didn't have to worry about streaks. Often, I thought about how great it would be if I were only vacuuming—then I would be so close to going home. Window washing was like the barren desert before the Promised Land.

Finally, I got to the vacuuming. Unfortunately, by this time I was already very tired and ready to be finished. So of course this activity required me to move large pieces of furniture and push around an old-school vacuum that felt more like a small sack of bricks. I reminisced about when I only had to wield a tiny dust rag or a paper towel. At least with the window washing and dusting, I didn't have a super loud machine roaring at me as I tried to gather my thoughts about all the other things I needed to accomplish yet that night.

I remember getting into my car exhausted every week, relieved to mark another task off my to-do list. Then, one particularly reflective evening, I realized how ridiculous my thought process was. The reality was that at some point in the evening, I was able to identify positive aspects of each task—just never while I was doing it. I wondered how much my attitude might change if I were a little more intentional about appreciating the good things in the moment, instead of looking forward or back at them. I decided to do a little mental experiment the following week.

As I pulled up to the house a week later, I could tell something was different about my attitude. I had already made up my mind to be intentional about this night. As I walked through the door and greeted the woman, I was reminded why I had started cleaning her house in the first place. She was such a beautiful soul, and her warmth and gratefulness for my service washed over me. In that moment, I was so happy to be there with her. Now for my true challenge—it was time to start working.

As I picked up my dust rag and started moving all the knick-knacks, I thought about how great it was that I didn't have to worry about streaks. I focused on how light everything was and even took a new interest in some of the items, wondering about the stories behind them. Before I knew it, the dusting was finished and I was on to the window washing.

As I worked on the windows and mirrors, I took extra pleasure in the fact that I didn't have to move a dang thing. It felt like the easiest task of my night, and I couldn't believe it when I was already halfway done with my work. I remember being shocked at how much faster everything seemed like it was going. Perhaps it was all in my mind, but it even seemed like the mirrors and windows had fewer streaks.

Now for the vacuuming . . . Unlike other weeks, I came into my final chore full of energy. I thought about what great exercise it was to move the furniture and push the heavy vacuum around. I loved that the sound of the vacuum provided great cover for me to hum a little tune that I could dance to as I polished off my work for the night. My enjoyment of the evening blew my mind.

I got into the car that night with a smile still on my face. It was truly a defining moment for me. I thought to myself, *This is how I want to live my life. I want to be the kind of person who intentionally soaks up the joy from every moment. No matter how busy I am or how bad things seem, I want to be able to find beauty in the dusting.*

AMBITIONS MEET REALITY

Now let's be real, as nice as that sounds, being positive all the time is pretty darn unrealistic—especially when you find yourself in a tunnel of darkness. When I think back on my naïveté in the car that night, I just shake my head. To consider that mundane housework ranked high on my list of awful things in life is now quite laughable. I clearly had no idea what I was in for down the road. Even so, I think I was onto something, which is why this story made it into the journal.

According to an article by Jennifer Hawthorne, humans have "anywhere from 12,000 to 60,000 thoughts per day." She goes on to share that according to research, "98 percent of them are exactly the same as the day before," and more importantly, "80 percent of our thoughts are negative" (Hawthorne 2014). Not only are we all hardwired to see the glass as half empty, these are the thoughts we have on replay for ourselves day after day.

Negative thinking is kind of like being on one of those moving walkways at the airport. If you stand still, you keep moving forward. Even just to stay in the same place, you have to turn around and walk in the opposite direction. And the only way to make any progress is to literally *jog* in the opposite direction. How exhausting does that sound when your tank is already empty? No wonder people tend to stick with the default of negative thinking. Maintaining a positive attitude goes against our natural tendencies, which is hard work, even under normal circumstances. So does that mean we should all just throw up our hands and give in to our inner pessimism? Of course not, but overcoming it does require self-discipline that is not unlike physical fitness.

Imagine a non-athlete training for a triathlon. In the beginning, the training process might feel overwhelming, but over time strength and endurance are built. Remember, we repeat the same thoughts to ourselves every day, so if we want to get out of the rut of negative thinking, we need to strap on our running shoes and start wearing some new paths.

In his book *Tribe of Mentors*, author Timothy Ferriss paraphrases a thought from one of his personal mentors, Dr. Jim Loehr. Ferriss writes, "The power broker in your life is the voice that no one ever hears. How well you revisit the tone and content of your private voice is what determines the quality of your life. It is the master storyteller, and the stories we tell ourselves are our reality" (Ferriss 2017). I tend to underestimate the power of that inner voice and my ability to shape it, so Ferriss's thought process hit home in a real way as I was training to run a half marathon ten years ago.

RESTING IN THE DOWNHILLS

Fitness has always been important to me. I was not genetically gifted with a fast metabolism, and I love food, so I have also needed to cultivate an interest in exercise. However, if I had to pick my least favorite fitness activity of all time, it would be running. Some people really enjoy it. I am inclined to believe those people are a little bit crazy. In all fairness, the problem is likely that I am not very good at it. My jogging pace could probably be considered more like spirited walking.

You may be wondering what in the world convinced me that training for a half marathon would be a good idea. That is a totally reasonable question—what the heck was I thinking? Well, I mostly did it as an act of self-discipline, but I remember with brutal clarity the start of the whole process. My first few runs felt very much like subjecting myself to cruel and unusual torture. I would set short-term goals for myself, like "If I can just make it to that mailbox, then I can walk to the next stop sign." Over time, the stretches of jogging became longer, and the walking breaks shorter and more infrequent.

I remember the day I set out having realized the time had arrived for me to eliminate all the walking breaks. Even though I was in much better cardiovascular shape than when I had started my training, the idea still seemed daunting to me. My body was technically capable, but my mind was not fully convinced. My inner coach kept telling me that I was not cut out for this challenge.

Deep into my run, I came to a familiar corner where I had become accustomed to taking a walking break. My anxiety spiked. "There is no way I'm going to make it through this whole run," I thought. I could feel my heart beating out of my chest, and my lungs burned as I tried to suck in more air. I was just about to throw in the towel and start walking when I noticed for the first time that I wasn't very far from a downhill section.

At that moment something clicked for me. I can't fully explain it because the physical impact of it still baffles me to this day, but something shifted in my mind. I realized that even though I couldn't stop running, I could reframe the downhill as my place to rest. All of a sudden, there seemed to be more oxygen. My heart rate began to slow, and my anxiety subsided even though I was still jogging. The only thing that had changed was my attitude. This moment became a pivotal point in my training, but it also had a profound impact on my life.

What I discovered is that where I focused my attention mattered. I have a friend whose cross-country coach used to tell her that when breathing hurt, she should focus on how strong her legs were, or when her legs were giving out, she could focus on how her arms felt fine. If her arms got tired, she could focus on how she wasn't as chilly as before she started the race.

Sometimes you don't have the option of making the pain go away. In those moments, it helps to focus on something that doesn't hurt as much. Kyle and I found a way to shift our focus when we started a page in our journal for capturing silver linings.

It was one way that we intentionally focused our minds on seeking the positive aspects of what we had.

GRANDMA'S DOLLS

During the same timeframe as my marathon training, I was working a full-time job, studying for my MBA in the evenings, and trying to balance a number of other commitments. Once again, I was on the edge of burnout with little time to rest or recharge. What I realized after my running epiphany was that some of my activities were "downhill" moments for me. For example, once a week I would go to my grandma's house to help her with a special project.

My grandma was an avid doll collector. I'm not talking about a creepy little room in her basement with a bunch of old dolls. Her collection was massive and totally impressive. She had been accumulating for over sixty years, and her whole house was full of beautiful dolls in their original boxes. After my grandpa died, she even converted their garage into an amazing doll room with floor-to-ceiling displays of her special treasures. My project was to help her catalog her enormous collection by photographing and documenting thousands of dolls. It was technically another commitment on my already busy schedule, but once I reframed it as an opportunity to recharge, it made everything else seem a little less overwhelming.

The Big Picture is that sometimes life doesn't give you the option to quit moving; you just have to keep going. In grief, sometimes putting one foot in front of the other can feel unbearable, but no matter how grueling the path, there are always downhills. For us, journaling was a downhill. We framed it up as a chance to recharge even though it required some work for us to talk our thoughts out and write them down. Once we identified journaling as a downhill moment, it became less exhausting and we were able to soak much more rest out of the activity.

NO REGRETS

This kind of mindset shift has another beautiful upside. It helps us fully appreciate the things we have while we have them. Take, for example, my weekly task of helping my grandma archive her doll collection. We finished the project in 2013, but I had no idea that in early 2017 I would have to say goodbye to this amazing woman. I remember looking back through all the photos I had taken of her during our weekly visits. I had so many beautiful memories of my time with her. As I stood at her memorial, I could smile through the tears because I knew that I had truly cherished the time we had together. It was such a bittersweet moment, but I can honestly say the sweet outweighed the bitter.

This concept of appreciating the good in what you have while you have it is broadly applicable. In the final episode of the show *The Office*, Ed Helms's character, Andy Bernard, says, "I wish there was a way to know you're in 'the good old days' before you've actually left them" (Kwapis 2013). This was delivered in a comedic context, but his words resonate. It is much easier to look back and see the good in a situation after it has passed than to see it in the moment.

Life naturally occurs in cycles. We are constantly dealing with endings and new beginnings. Sometimes those things are fun and exciting, like new relationships, and sometimes they are incredibly painful, like saying goodbye to something or someone you love. Even in the most difficult situations, you can have closure in knowing you didn't take what you had for granted while you had it.

THE SINGLE LADY

I once knew a woman who deeply wanted to find her soul mate, but her life didn't go as planned. She found herself single long after all of her friends had settled down and started having children. Instead of feeling lonely or jealous of other couples, she decided to focus on all the positive aspects of being single. She spent tons of time with her family. She invested in her career and her education. She mentored young women and traveled spontaneously. She spoiled her friends' children. She soaked up all the joy from her singleness, although it lasted far longer than she would have chosen. However, when she finally met the man of her dreams, she was able to walk down the aisle to the next season of her life with no regrets.

Appreciating the positive aspects of what you have keeps you from becoming consumed by the negatives, even if the situation is something you never would have chosen for yourself. Appreciation leads to contentment and joy regardless of your circumstances.

THE POWER OF ATTENTION

So what are we really getting at here? Are we saying that positive thinking is the answer to the darkness? No. Honestly, it's not that simple. A positive attitude is helpful, but that alone is not enough. In his book *Happiness by Design*, Paul Dolan talks about how attempting to change the way you think is often a recipe for failure, especially if it is not rooted in reality. Instead he encourages people to be mindful of where they are directing their attention.

According to Dolan, "What you attend to drives your behavior and determines your happiness. Attention is the glue that holds your life together." We have already discussed how we all tend to fixate on the negative. Dolan believes the key to happiness is to "allocate your attention as best as you can" (Dolan 2014).

Let's go back to my example of the single woman. Her situation would have been very different if she had just tried to "think positive thoughts" as she endured her singleness. Instead, she shifted her attention to the things that made her happy about her singleness, which then influenced her behavior. In turn, this thought process also took her focus off the fact that she didn't have the romantic relationship she desired. Dolan says, "Changing behavior and enhancing happiness is as much about withdrawing attention from the negative as it is about attending to the positive" (Dolan 2014).

So often in life we are met with circumstances we wouldn't choose but we don't have the power to change. We are stuck in a tunnel of darkness, but that does not mean we are powerless. We can choose to look for glimmers of light. We can choose to reframe the stories we tell ourselves, and we can choose how we allocate our attention. These are the choices that will help us gracefully navigate the uncharted pathways that lie ahead.

CHAPTER 3

BETTY'S PERSPECTIVE

Twists and Turns

*This is not what we planned,
but it can still be beautiful.*

THE WRONG TURN

In early July 2009, I had just completed a master's degree and helped wrap up a significant project as part of my fundraising role at the University of Northwestern, St. Paul. In the next few months I would be relocating and starting my corporate career, so I decided to celebrate by taking a spontaneous trip to Ireland with one of my closest friends.

My dad immediately forced me to watch the movie *Taken*, which is about two girls who are kidnapped by a gang of human traffickers while traveling abroad. The film was appropriately terrifying. However, I was resolute in my decision to go, so my friend and I carefully started planning our trip. Our goal was to see as much of Ireland as possible. We liked the safety of a tour group, but did not want the structure of a traditional guided tour. We settled on a hybrid approach in which we would get our own rental car and meet up each night at the same hotels as the tour group.

The trip was filled with breathtaking sights, hearty laughter, and incredible conversations, but my most poignant memory took place on the road to Killarney. I should start by establishing that driving on the opposite side of the car and the road in an unfamiliar place is a complete mind-trip. Now, add in a slightly deranged GPS device with a hilarious accent. Our time in the car was split evenly between white-knuckled terror and laughing until we had tears running down our faces.

One particular evening we were headed toward our hotel in Killarney, but our GPS device had clearly lost its mind. It kept telling us to turn off in the middle of cornfields. Don't get me wrong, we were up for making memories, but not the kind that involved a tow truck. We finally decided that the best solution would be to embrace the adventure by turning off the GPS and finding our own way to the hotel.

About two minutes after we made this bold decision, we came to a fork in the road. On the map, Killarney seemed to be straight ahead of us, but forward was not one of our options. We had to choose between a left or a right. These are the types of moments I dread. I am a planner so I can avoid moments like these in which there is no clear, right answer. My friend just looked at me and said, "Well, fearless leader?" With all the false confidence I could manufacture, I boldly said, "We go left!"

A few kilometers down the road, we came around a bend that revealed one of the most spectacular views I have ever seen. Before us was a picturesque stone pier with a magnificent view of the sunset over the ocean. Cars filled a small parking lot as people lined up along the pier to watch the sunset. It was clearly a sought-after view. We joined the onlookers and stayed until all the beautiful colors had faded away to dusk. We couldn't believe the good fortune that had led us to this particular spot at the perfect time.

As we headed back to the car, we could tell from the voices around us that many were locals. This would be a perfect opportunity to ask for directions! We stopped a friendly-looking individual and explained that we were trying to get from Dublin to Killarney. "Ah," he said with a charming Irish accent, "Killarney is behind you. You should have made a right at the turn back there."

Crazy that one of my favorite moments of the whole trip was the result of a wrong turn. Sitting at the fork in the road with no idea which way to go had felt so chaotic to me. If I had known Killarney was to the right, I never would have chosen to go the wrong way. I guess it's for the best that we don't always know and that we can't always control everything. Sometimes a direction we never would have chosen for ourselves provides a spectacular view we otherwise would have missed.

A TRAGIC TWIST

OK, so the wrong turn in Ireland made for a cute story, but what happens when your whole life takes a wrong turn? I'm not talking about a pleasant little diversion but a world-wrecking twist you never saw coming. If losing our daughter taught us anything, it was how little control we really have in life. We can make plans, but we have to hold them with open hands because we don't really know what tomorrow has in store.

If you are like me, this approach probably sounds a bit terrifying, but it is surprisingly freeing. If we got to choose everything, life would lack depth. Who would choose for bad things to happen? Nobody wants a silver lining—we all just want the sun. Trying to avoid pain is natural, but darkness creates contrast so we can better appreciate the light. Think about it—all light and no dark is just a whiteout. Contrast is what exposes beauty.

BABY SHOES

My mom always wanted to have a large family. Before she and my father were married, she had a hope chest full of baby shoes. She had no idea the challenges that would lie ahead. Shortly after they got married, they became pregnant with their first child. Three months later, my mom miscarried. This would be the first of many miscarriages, each with its own unique cause.

The miscarriages became so common that people no longer celebrated with her when she shared she was pregnant. Nobody wanted to get their hopes up until, at long-last, my mom gave birth to my oldest sister. Due to high blood pressure, my mom was admitted to the Intensive Care Unit, where she was not able to keep the baby with her. Mom recalls through tears that she discharged herself from the hospital so she could go home and care for her precious little girl.

This would not be the end of her struggle with miscarriages, but she was eventually able to have three more children, including me. The trials she went through created a sense of awe for the miracle of childbirth and made each new baby even more precious to her and my father. My mom has always said she would love to have had more children, but if you ask her today, she will tell you that her life is "full of beautiful jewels."

She now has four children and twelve grandchildren, including Ella. Not only did her miscarriages give her a deeper appreciation for her family, they made her a better mother. They also unknowingly prepared her to support me through my loss. Though our circumstances were different, my mom understood the deep pain of losing a child.

WALTER'S STORY

Sometimes the life-changing twist is not the loss of a child but the loss of an idea. We know a young family who found out they were pregnant with their second child when their daughter was only nine months old. Although they had initially planned to have their children farther apart, the expecting parents quickly became excited to watch their little ones grow up so close in age.

At the beginning of their twenty-week anatomy scan, they found out they were having a little boy, which made them absolutely giddy! However, by the end of that ultrasound, their world would be turned upside down. They came to learn that their baby had two heart defects and that he also had Trisomy 21, commonly known as Down syndrome.

They were devastated. Their beautiful vision of a typical life for their son and family had vanished. They feared that their daughter wouldn't have a normal relationship with her brother, that he would need multiple surgeries, that he would look different, that he wouldn't meet his milestones on time, that he would live with them forever and not have a meaningful adult life, that their family wouldn't be able to do normal things like go on vacation. They worried that their lives would be completely disrupted.

When Walter was born, he did change their world, but for the better. Walter has physical features that are common in individuals with Down syndrome, but he also looks like his sister and he is absolutely adorable. He is delayed in meeting his milestones, but when he does meet one, the whole family celebrates fiercely. They are still able to take family vacations and, although they would be happy to have Walter with them forever, they are encouraged that he may one day be able to hold a meaningful job and live a relatively independent adult life.

Overall their journey has been challenging but rewarding. In the words of Walter's mother:

"Our lives have been disrupted and I am so incredibly thankful for that. We have slowed down. We are more understanding and empathetic towards others. We celebrate the small things more often. We don't get so worked up about situations out of our control or when things don't go exactly as we planned. We laugh a lot and experience so much joy in watching our kids' relationship."

Adverse circumstances can be an incredible catalyst for growth. Walter's family is a perfect example. This path is not what they would have envisioned for themselves, but look at how their lives have been enriched. Also consider the ripple effect—Kyle and I noted their story in our journal because it inspired us. Now here you are reading about it. When you go through something challenging, it can have a positive impact not only on your life but also the lives of those around you.

VIBRANT STARS

Before we lost Ella, we never fully understood what an amazing support system we had. It was like a giant, invisible net that we never could have fully comprehended until we needed it. Like confident trapeze artists, we never anticipated falling, but nothing compared to the feeling of that net flexing around as we landed on it—hard. It gave us a deeper appreciation of something we had all along even though we couldn't see it.

Consider the difference between a night sky over a city filled with lights and noise, and the same sky over a field in the middle of nowhere. Even though the contents of the sky have not changed, in the field, with no other lights around, you have an incredible view of the stars. Our lives with Ella had been like living in the city, but in our grief, we stumbled into a dark field and discovered our own blanket of stars.

We often say losing Ella gave us a front-row seat to see the goodness in other people. That is an understatement. Our neighbors tied pink ribbons on every mailbox in our subdivision. They hosted a BBQ to raise money to help cover our funeral expenses and set up a meal train to provide us with food for over a month after she died. Ella's daycare had her most recent artwork professionally framed for us. Friends and co-workers flew in from Minnesota, Michigan, Arizona, Georgia, Tennessee, and many other places to attend her funeral. People cleaned our house, cut our grass, sent flowers, helped us prepare for the memorial service, gave thoughtful gifts, wrote poems, created beautiful artwork, lit heart-shaped lanterns in our front yard, provided services for free, and wrote special messages to us via Facebook and email. People sent cards, money, and gift certificates. Some of our friends even set up a GoFundMe page and circulated it on social media. It brought in $17,418. Some of the donations were from complete strangers who were touched by our story.

Even as I reflect on these absolutely incredible gestures, tears roll down my face. After the dust settled, we had hundreds of thank you cards to write, so we decided on a single message:

> Ella Marie was a perfect gift! She brought so much joy and light into our lives that losing her truly felt like losing the sunshine. Although nothing could have prepared us for this darkness, the love and generosity of those around us has been like a sky full of vibrant stars. We are overwhelmed and grateful for all the support we've received. Thank you for being a bright spot in this difficult time. Like the stars, nothing completely removes the darkness, but we are awestruck by the beautiful reminders that we are not alone.

Just because your view is different from what you would have chosen, that doesn't mean it can't be beautiful. Even apart from the amazing support we received, our loss provided us with a much broader perspective. When you experience such a low valley, it makes the next mountaintop seem even higher.

STRONGER THAN YOU REALIZE

There is no way around it—life is going to deal you some twists and turns that are outside of your control. Some of them will be relatively inconsequential, and some will completely unravel all your plans. People often comment about the strength Kyle and I have shown in the face of our tragedy. You know, if someone had asked me before I lost Ella if I was strong enough to handle it, I would have said no.

It reminds me of an experience I had at the gym. I had told my personal trainer, Briana Swanson, that I wanted to set a goal for myself of being able to do an unassisted pull-up. Just for reference, I was always the girl in gym class who couldn't even last for five seconds on the flexed arm hang. I deeply relate to the T-Rex when it comes to muscle distribution in my body.

In any case, over the next eight weeks I focused on my training. Bri incorporated a number of upper-body moves into my workouts and I spent an exasperating amount of time feeling weak and sore. After two months, Bri asked me how my progress was going on the full-body-weight pull-up. I told her that I was still nowhere near my goal. She asked me to grab the bar and give it a shot.

I was willing to oblige her to prove my point. Well, imagine my surprise when my chin went up over the bar. I was completely shocked. It felt like magic. I surprised myself with how much strength I had built over time.

Getting back to our grief—sometimes I think people believe there was something innately special about Kyle and me that helped us emerge from our tragedy with such a positive outlook. I'm going to let you in on a little secret—it wasn't magic. It was practice. It came from looking for the good in many smaller, less-than-ideal circumstances along the way. It's also something we must continue practicing.

No matter what the situation, we firmly believe that the good can outweigh the bad. When life deals us a crazy plot twist we can't change, we look for the glimmer of light in our crazy-dark tunnel and keep moving forward. It can be tempting to get caught in the trap of wishing for something different, but the truth is that the grass isn't always greener on the other side.

Surrounded by Darkness
Grappling with Heavy Emotions

THE MIDDLE OF THE TUNNEL

There comes a point in every tunnel where you are farthest from the light on both ends. For many, when faced with extreme grief, it can be easy to get stuck in the darkest part of the tunnel. It is totally normal to face very real and very raw emotions when grieving a loss. Feelings like guilt, jealousy, anger, bitterness, fear, and anxiety are real and need to be acknowledged. The next few thoughts and stories offer insight on how to keep from spiraling in the dark.

Comparison

You can't compare your empty to someone else's full.

THE COMPARISON GAME

When I learn about someone else's experiences, I often find myself comparing their stories to instances in my own life. I think this kind of comparison is natural as a way to find relatable similarities. By reflecting back on my own experiences, I'm better able to understand the emotions and challenges others might be facing.

After we lost Ella, I started comparing the losses and tragedies of others to the loss of my daughter. This comparison was not just for the purpose of empathy. Regardless of the situation, I was always able to find a reason why my loss was worse or more difficult to deal with. It didn't even occur to me that I was doing this until I found myself using conflicting logic with two similar losses.

The first experience involved a couple who never really had the opportunity to meet their child. Their emotions were very similar to those Betty and I had experienced; however, I couldn't help but think of the thirteen months we spent with our daughter. We invested a year in learning about this little person. We watched her grow and cheered her on at every milestone. We knew all about her little personality and how she smelled. Long after her death, we would wake up in the middle of the night listening for her cry. This family didn't have all those memories to reflect back on, so my experience should be more difficult to deal with, right?

A few months later we met a couple who had lost a teenager. We were deeply impacted by their story. They had clearly experienced very similar emotions despite our children being so different in age. Once again, as I was reflecting on their story I started comparing their situation to my loss. I was thinking how they had the opportunity to spend more than ten years with their child, which made our thirteen months with Ella seem so short. My loss seemed more difficult because I missed out on all those years.

Suddenly I remembered the couple who never saw their child grow. At that moment I realized the flaw in my logic. I couldn't have it both ways. My situation couldn't always be the worst-case scenario. The amount of time you had with a loved one doesn't make the loss any easier or harder—the situation is simply different.

Dealing with loss is awful, regardless of whether it's a child, spouse, friend, parent, or grandparent. Trying to compare these losses doesn't help. Each person is dealing with their own situation and how the pain is relative to what they've experienced. Everyone has their "worst thing." Instead of wasting energy trying to figure out how one tragedy stacks up to another, let's allow our scars to help us become even more empathetic to those around us.

TRADING LIVES

One evening not long after Ella's memorial, Betty and I were taking a walk around the neighborhood. If you've met my wife, you know she loves to ask questions and is genuinely interested in your response. She asked me, "Would you trade lives with any of our friends?" The question seemed reasonable considering we had just lost our daughter and our lives had been flipped on end. I didn't answer right away. I wanted to give a fair and honest response.

We have a lot of great people in our lives and our friends have a lot of good things going for them. We have friends with beautiful families, impressive careers, lovely homes, and so on. As I thought about the question and thought about the different people in our lives, finding enviable things was easy, but the question wasn't to pick and choose all the best things. I was asked if there was one couple I would trade lives with. Despite just losing our only child and feeling totally broken, there was still much to love about my life. It was the result of a lifetime of prioritization and decisions I had made along the way. To switch lives with someone else would mean being happy with all the decisions they had made. So, my answer to Betty's question was "No, I wouldn't trade lives with anyone else."

Every day is full of choices, and every choice we make comes with sacrifice in another area. Time, money, and energy are just a few of our resources, and every day we make choices regarding the best way to utilize them. It's easy to look at what someone else has and desire it but not think about what they may have sacrificed to get it. Their life may be full in that area but empty in another because of how they have chosen to allocate their resources. You can't compare your empty to someone else's full.

Understanding your goals and priorities will help you ensure you're making decisions to achieve the result you desire. But what if your desire is to avoid tragedy? The truth is, bad stuff can impact anyone. A few months prior, someone might have wanted to trade lives with us. How could they have known that we would lose our daughter? You don't get to cherry-pick the good things out of life. You take what comes at you and make the best decisions you can, and then love what you have. Contentment itself is enviable.

A couple years after Ella died, one of Betty's friends was reflecting on our relationship and she said, "You guys are so lucky!" We were surprised that anyone would say that about us. Who in their right mind would call us lucky after what we have been through?

However, she wasn't looking at an area in which we were empty. She was looking at an area in which we were full. And she is right—we are lucky! Our marriage has been refined by fire, and we appreciate our time together more than ever now.

LIFE IS SHORT

When we look back at our time with Ella, we're thankful we didn't take it for granted. Despite not knowing we would only have her for a short time, we didn't let having a baby slow us down. Fitting so much activity into Ella's first year allowed us to look back without regret and know we wouldn't do anything differently. We'll always have those precious memories of our time with her.

One recurring theme in our journal is the importance of making the best use of the time you have. If you're going to spend resources on something eventually, don't procrastinate. You might as well enjoy the maximum benefit of whatever it is by doing it sooner rather than later. Besides, there are no guarantees that it will still be an option tomorrow. Putting it off could cause you to miss the window all together.

After Ella passed, Betty's parents decided they would move back to St. Louis. They felt they missed out on a lot of Ella's life and wanted to be able to spend more time with their grandchildren and future grandchildren. Before they could move, they needed to finish their house in Galesville, Wisconsin, to put it on the market.

When they originally moved to Galesville, they purchased a one-hundred-eighty-year-old home that needed a complete overhaul. They proceeded to gut the house and redo every wall. For the first year, they lived in an active construction zone. Once all the big, important projects were finished, they decided to take a break from their renovation efforts. The house was about 95 percent complete. They lived in it like that for the next four years.

In order to receive the maximum resale value from the house when they sold it, they pushed through and finished the last 5 percent. Unfortunately, it was just in time for someone else to enjoy living in a 100 percent completed home. They still joke about how nice it was those last few weeks when they could sit in their finished sunroom and appreciate the view.

Maximizing the benefit from effort is why both Betty and I decided to get our MBAs early in our careers. We knew it was something that we would want to do eventually, and we would never have more time to fit them in. Finishing earlier would only assist us in our careers as we would be able to apply the knowledge gained for a longer period of time.

This same maximization concept is why I have no issue receiving gifts early and why I also highly recommend you do the same if given the opportunity. Why can't I be surprised NOW with this birthday or Christmas present and enjoy it for a longer period of time? Life is short. Nobody is promised tomorrow, and although we want to make choices that will hold up in the long run, being able to fully enjoy each day is important.

CALCULATED RISK

In 2018, we were pregnant with our second daughter, Layne, and our son, Ryder, was about to turn one. In an effort to embrace the present, Betty and I decided to take some of the money we had been aggressively saving and make an investment that would bring value to us in the short-term. We started looking for lake property. Our vision was to buy a fixer-upper that would be a great place for us to spend time with family and make memories.

We discovered an A-frame cabin in a lake community called Innsbrook. The price was right and it seemed to have great bones. The only downside was that it hadn't been updated since the '70s and would require a lot of work. But, with Ryder about to turn one and Layne only six months from being born, I figured we had a great workforce on the way.

All joking aside, Betty and I both had had fond experiences at Innsbrook when we were younger and knew it would be a great place to take our kids as they grew. We got to work and quickly learned that there would be no simple projects. Forrest Gump always said, "Life is like a box of chocolates. You never know what you're gonna get." Starting a project at the cabin was no different. We would pull up the old carpet only to reveal rotted panels on the floor that we had to replace before moving forward. Even something as simple as painting a wall—hope you're ready to put on five coats!

Sometimes we would create our own projects, like when I flooded the upstairs bathroom and water dripped down through the ceiling into the kitchen. *Well, it looks like this carpet in the kitchen is ready to get pulled up tonight.* Every new challenge tested our patience and resolve. We gained lots of practice facing trials with good humor, and we learned a lot of new skills. The same thing happens in life, doesn't it? Challenges teach us, test us, and make us stronger. Adaptability is an important skill that is best learned through adversity.

ROCK BOTTOM

In her book *Option B*, Sheryl Sandberg says, "I learned that when life pulls you under, you can kick against the bottom, break the surface, and breathe again" (Sandberg and Grant 2017). Losing Ella was our rock bottom. When you are that far down, it is easy to fall into the trap of comparing the rocks, but comparison is a flawed and fruitless game. Finding the silver lining in someone else's cloud is always easier than seeing the light in your own storm.

After we lost Ella, we heard from countless people, "I don't know how you go on" or "I wouldn't be able to get out of bed." If anything, losing Ella made us realize how precious life is. We don't want to waste it. Even at our lowest low, we still had a lot of good in our lives. We had each other, we had great friends and family surrounding us, and we had a good future to look forward to. Focusing on those things helped us push up toward the surface.

We don't know your situation. Perhaps you don't have the support system we had. The point is that you have something, even if it's just a hard surface to push off of. It is hard to stay down when you are looking up. One thing you can know for sure is that you will have a unique perspective to offer to other people in similar situations down the road.

Theodore Roosevelt has been attributed with saying, "Comparison is the thief of joy," and whether or not he actually said it, the sentiment rings true. Comparison is not always accurate or helpful because you don't have the full picture. Comparing your empty to someone else's full is a recipe for discontentment, which can breed bitterness. Instead, let whatever you have experienced make you more empathetic to others and more grateful for the good in what you have. Bitterness cannot coexist with gratefulness.

Big, Ugly Feelings

*For the rest of my life there will be a part of me
that is sad every day, and that's OK.*

WATCHING THE NEWS

One time we were talking to another bereaved parent and she mentioned that it's hard for her to watch the news. You so frequently see stories about parents who are not prioritizing the health and well-being of their kids. She said it just makes her so angry that there are people out there in this world who do not deserve to be parents while incredibly loving and caring people like her have their child ripped from them for no reason. It's not fair.

She's right. It's not fair. These types of stories are frustrating to watch regardless of having lost a child. But when you've experienced a great loss or heartbreak, your perspective changes and a frustrating topic becomes much more personal. Like the pain from an exposed, raw nerve, our emotional response to the situation is heightened.

Anger is a completely normal response to trauma, along with a whole bunch of other negative emotions. Feelings like fear, sadness, panic, bitterness, anxiety, loneliness, and depression are all very common. Trying to fight against them, deny them, or cram them down is not practical or helpful. In fact, it often makes matters worse.

GRIEF IS A HOT MESS

Before our tragedy, I had heard of the five stages of grief. I figured the grieving process probably followed some sort of general pattern. I was wrong. Grief is a complex bundle of emotions, and it is different for every person. Not only that, but you can find yourself bouncing back and forth between different "stages" that you've already been through.

One thing I can say from personal experience is that grief is not linear. Sometimes you go from crying to laughter in an instant. Or you will have a bunch of days that seem to be getting progressively better and then all of a sudden you have a wave of hard days. The only thing you can count on is the lack of a pattern.

Even though experiencing a loss can feel like your world is shattered in an instant, it takes time to fully process all the implications. Grief unravels differently for each person. Even though Betty and I are similar people who experienced the same loss, our grieving was different. We had different emotions that hit us at unique times. Different things were helpful and triggering to each of us. For example, I remember right after Ella's death, I frequently wanted to watch videos and look at pictures of her. Seeing and hearing her helped me feel close to her, even though she was gone. Betty had the opposite response. Seeing the pictures and hearing the videos made her even more homesick for our daughter.

To make matters even more complicated, men and women tend to be wired differently. Men often to relate to one another shoulder to shoulder, like sitting at the bar watching a football or hockey game together. Women, on the other hand, tend to communicate face to face and share more freely about their emotions. I don't mean to overgeneralize because each person is unique. We all fall somewhere on this communication spectrum. Each of us has varying degrees of comfort and ability to express what we're thinking and feeling with others.

At the end of the day, it is important to find ways to share about the trauma we've experienced. Martin E.P. Seligman, author of *Flourish,* talks about working with patients struggling with post-traumatic stress disorder (PTSD). He says, "Bottling up trauma likely leads to worsening of physical and psychological symptoms, so soldiers are encouraged to tell the story of the trauma" (Seligman 2011). He refers to this as "creating a trauma narrative." Even for people who struggle with communication, it's healthy to tell the story of what happened.

Having a support system in place, if possible, can help when tragedy strikes. That system of support can look different for everyone and may include parents, siblings, friends, a support group, a grief counselor, or others. Regardless of who is providing the support, the biggest benefit will come through self-awareness and honest communication.

Betty and I found that connecting with others who had experienced a similar loss was very helpful. Even if we weren't specifically talking about our grief, just knowing the other person understood the internal struggle was enough—building the relationship and knowing you're not alone can be powerful.

If nothing else, you can take comfort in the fact that you aren't doing it wrong. There isn't a right way. For us, communication, authenticity, self-awareness, and external support were really helpful. We recommend contacting a therapist, counselor, or even medical professional for help, especially if your feelings may be leading to detrimental or unhealthy behavior.

Going through a loss is awful. Reaching out for help is not a sign of weakness. In her book, *Daring Greatly,* Brené Brown says, "Vulnerability sounds like truth and feels like courage. Truth and courage aren't always comfortable, but they're never weakness"

(Brown 2015). I've learned that sometimes asking for help is the strongest thing I can do. Plus, having additional perspective can be helpful in providing grounding to deal with feelings like anger and guilt. Sometimes when we are overwhelmed with heavy emotions with no place to direct them, we end up turning them on others or even back on ourselves.

THE BLAME GAME

Whenever something goes wrong, it's easy to look for someone to blame. Sometimes there is clearly another person at fault, but other times we look for places to lay blame. Pointing the finger at someone else can be a way to try and cope with grief. Let's just state the obvious, blaming others doesn't fix the pain. The anger just makes it more difficult to heal and move on.

If you are like Betty and me, perhaps you tend to blame yourself when things go wrong. It is natural to think of what we could have done differently and create a narrative around how different choices would have changed the outcome. We questioned every choice we made with Ella and every action we could have taken.

The problem with this exercise is that there is no way to know what the impact of a different choice would have been. Or what new choices we would encounter in that alternate reality and how we would have responded. The bigger problem is that we can't actually change anything, so obsessing over what we might have done differently is not only futile, but can lead to deep, debilitating depression and self-doubt.

Although guilt is a natural reaction, it is not incredibly helpful. It is also not always accurate. Sometimes we take more responsibility for things than we should. When something terrible happens, it's important to remember that hindsight is twenty-twenty. If you had all the same information today that you wish you had in the past, you might have made a different set of choices. But it's still anyone's guess what the outcome would have been.

In the months that followed Ella's death, I struggled with the thought that "as her father, I had one job and it was to protect her." Instead, she ended up protecting me. After we found out Ella had a genetic mutation, Betty and I were both tested. It turns out I was the spontaneous anomaly who developed the mutation first and I passed it down to Ella. Even though it hasn't impacted me in the same way as it did her, the doctors tell me it is just a matter of time. The fact that they can now monitor my heart and know what to look for means that it won't kill me. My daughter saved my life.

One thing I know is that I never would have chosen this outcome for Ella. Whenever guilt creeps in, I can firmly remind myself of that. The choices that were made were the best I could have made with the information available. Also, there is no guarantee that a different decision would have changed the outcome. The best I can do is look for the things I learned to help make me a better father to my other children. Beyond that, there are too many factors outside of my control.

THE NIGHTMARES ARE REAL

If our loss did anything, it taught us how little control we have. One tiny chromosome can change everything. Unfortunately, this knowledge is less than comforting. When you realize how fragile life truly is, it's hard not to live in fear, which is the flip side of not taking a moment for granted. But after living through a nightmare, all other nightmares now seem more plausible. Sometimes this can keep people from moving forward, but one of the things we wrote in our journal was that "Most good things come with risk." You have to be willing to accept the risk to move forward, knowing that the good can outweigh the bad.

I remember when Betty found out she was pregnant with Ryder, and we were concerned about the pregnancy going smoothly. We were worried about him having the same heart condition as Ella. He had a 50/50 chance, but we opted to wait until after he was born to do the genetic testing since the information wouldn't change any decision we could make before he was born. Any risk the testing might cause to the pregnancy wasn't worth the extra bit of information at that time.

These fears can be paralyzing. They can make you want to hold onto what you have even more tightly, but what we have found is that this response is actually counterintuitive. Dealing with fear and anxiety is like one of those Chinese finger puzzles. The more you fight against them, the more they grip you. The only way to free yourself is to push your fingers toward each other.

When facing nightmares, sometimes you have to do something counterintuitive. Like in trying to avoid a car crash, sometimes you have to turn left to go right. When a car begins to spin or skid, you need to turn the opposite direction. It doesn't make intuitive sense to turn into the skid, but in doing so, you can correct it and regain control. The same is often true in life; if you let your emotions make your decisions, they can put you in a dangerous position. It is better to have a calculated approach for controlling the fear.

An Australian physician named Claire Weekes was a pioneer in identifying and treating anxiety. She found that fighting it doesn't work. Weekes said, "Fear starts a vicious feedback loop between the mind and the body. They get stuck in a fear cycle. You are in a state because you are frightened of yourself, frightened of the dreadful feeling of fear, frightened of your own symptoms, mental and physical which seem to have consumed you." In her book *Self-Help for Your Nerves*, her solution for ending this cycle involves the following four steps:

1. Face—Acknowledge your feelings and don't run from them.
2. Accept—Accept that what you are feeling is anxiety.
3. Float—Let your emotions float by you—observe them, but separate yourself.

4.   Let Time Pass—Don't be impatient with the discomfort, just let it play out in its own time (Weekes 1995).

Betty and I have found it really helpful to take a step back sometimes and separate ourselves from our feelings. We often refer to this as "stepping behind the waterfall," thanks to life coach Kirsten Parker. It is just a way of taking inventory without letting our feelings completely run the show. We don't try to stop them. We just watch them as they crash down in front of us and analyze what might be driving them.

The point here is that there is no way to get around all the big, heavy feelings that come with grief. Acknowledging them is very important, but they don't get the power to control us. Frank Herbert, author of *Dune*, says it this way: "I will face my fear. I will permit it to pass over me and through me. And when it has gone past, I will turn the inner eye to see its path. Where the fear has gone there will be nothing. Only I will remain" (Herbert 2019). We are more resilient now than ever before, but that doesn't mean we're not sad.

THE HIDDEN EMOTION

Unlike some of the other negative emotions, such as anger and bitterness, sadness can be a little easier to hide. There is also social pressure to bury sadness. Everyone wants us to be OK. It makes others much more comfortable if they feel like we are doing well and moving on, so we tend to try and soften the edges of our sadness.

Author and speaker Nora McInerny has a very popular TED talk on this subject called *We Don't "Move On" from Grief. We Move Forward with It*. She talks about how tragedy marks us and changes us permanently, just as much as joy-filled experiences do. She says, "We don't look at the people around us experiencing life's joys and tell them to 'move on,' do we?" She jokes about how we don't send a card of congratulations on a beautiful new baby, and then five years later think, "Geez, another birthday party? Get over it" (McInerny 2019).

McInerny goes on to explain that grief is one of those things that changes you. It is not a moment in time. It's not a broken bone that heals. It is chronic, and since it cannot be fixed, the best thing we can do is help each other remember. She refers to grief as a "multi-tasking emotion" that allows for sadness and happiness. She says that "a grieving person is going to laugh again and smile again . . . they are going to move forward, but that doesn't mean that they've moved on" (McInerny 2019).

For the rest of my life, there will be a part of me that is sad every day, and that's OK. It's not overwhelming in a sense that I cannot have happiness, but it still is here to stay. I don't feel like my sadness is an emotion I need to "hurry along," just like I would never try to "hurry along" joy. The positive and negative emotions can intermingle. The sadness is a constant reminder of how much I loved my daughter and how much she will continue to be missed. I still find happiness in knowing Ella, experiencing Ryder's and Layne's lives, loving my wife, and living life to the fullest.

ALL THE BIG FEELINGS

In an effort to comfort us, people would often say things like, "Ella would want you to move on and be happy." That sentiment did not resonate with us. She was just a baby. In one of the first pages of our journal, Betty wrote, "It's not fair to Ella for me to put the weight of my choice to be a good spouse, and eventually mother, on her—that's on me." We decided that we wanted Ella's legacy to make us the best versions of ourselves, and it has.

Even though ugly feelings are a natural response to trauma, they don't have to keep us from moving forward. When we start to feel stuck in the darkness, we can remember that we are not without power. All the uncomfortable emotions are just as valid as any other emotion, and the negative emotions can ride the bus—they just don't get to *drive* the bus. At the end of the day, moving forward is not dishonoring to the one you lost. Learning from your experience and allowing it to shape you for the better is part of how you carry your loved one with you.

Part 3

Light after Dark
Adjusting to the New Normal

EMERGING FROM THE TUNNEL

You know that feeling after your eyes have adjusted to darkness and then someone turns on a light? It can be downright painful. Even the smallest amount of light can seem shockingly bright. Emerging from the middle of the tunnel is like that. Honestly, it is part of what keeps people stuck in darkness. Exposure to light creates a sense of discomfort. These next few chapters talk about some of that transition out of darkness.

Compassion Heals

Being angry and bitter doesn't change anything,
it just makes everyone around you miserable.

THE ANGRY FATHER

One time Kyle and I crossed paths with another bereaved parent who seemed very stuck in his anger. He told us about how one day at work he encountered a coworker in the breakroom who was crying. She quickly apologized to him and explained that she was upset over a breakup with her significant other. She qualified that she knew it was nothing like what he and his wife been through. He looked at her and responded, "Yeah, you're in here crying because you broke up with your boyfriend. Try losing a kid." He shared this story with us as if we would be supportive and proud of him for delivering a healthy dose of well-needed perspective.

My stomach sank as I thought of how that poor girl must have felt. She was going through something that was clearly very difficult for her, and instead of having the support of another person who understood what it felt like to need a safe place for an emotional breakdown, she was met with a brick wall and a huge dose of guilt. The sad reality of the situation is that the very thing the girl wanted was something that the angry father had—a committed partner.

Think of how differently the situation could have played out if the angry father had shown a little more empathy. Instead of causing his coworker to feel shame over her pain, he could have provided encouragement that changed the course of her day. Perhaps it might also have led him to hug his wife a little more tightly after work that night.

As we discussed in the comparison chapter, we are all much better at pointing out the good in what other people have compared to us. It's worth the extra energy to flip that around. Everyone's story can help us better appreciate the good in what we have. Instead of letting difficult things harden us, we can let them make us even more sensitive and compassionate to those around us.

NO CRYING IN MEXICO

Warning: This section provides details about our daughter's story, which could be triggering. Feel free to skip ahead to the next section.

Back in 2017, we had scheduled a trip to an all-inclusive adults-only resort in Mexico with Kyle's parents. My mom was planning to come into town to watch Ella so we could have our first getaway since she had been born. Shortly before that trip is when Ella started wheezing and we decided to take her into the hospital. After things snowballed and she was admitted to the pediatric cardiac ICU (PICU), we ended up rescheduling our trip to push it out. All indicators were that Ella was on a track to a full recovery, but we needed to give her a little time to bounce back.

The new timing of the trip seemed like it would work out really well because our updated departure was scheduled for the day after Kyle's thirtieth birthday. What better way to kick off a new decade than soaking up some sun on the beach? Little did we know the events that would transpire on Kyle's birthday. We had no idea that it would be our last day to wake up with our baby girl.

I remember standing in complete shock in the hospital room moments after she died. My world had been turned upside down, and I had no idea what to do. I just wanted to run away. Fortunately, my bags were already packed. Kyle and I ended up making the controversial decision to move forward with our trip.

The next day I was in a total haze. I felt completely numb as we waited for our plane in the airport. I distinctly remember, during our flight, hitting a patch of extreme turbulence that would normally have freaked me out, but I remained completely calm. The thought of dying no longer scared me. It was surreal.

As we boarded the shuttle to the resort, some friendly passengers asked us where we were from. This started some lighthearted conversation until all of a sudden one of them asked if we had any children. I immediately broke down in tears. My husband gently put his arm around me as everyone in the shuttle sat in stunned silence. He explained that we had just lost our only child the day before, and everyone's eyes got a little bigger. They were all incredibly understanding and supportive after given the context, but this same scenario played out multiple times throughout our trip.

I remember sitting out by the pool one day and thinking about all the implications of my new reality. I couldn't control the tears as they rolled down my face. Another woman noticed my distress and came over to make sure I was OK. I broke down as I explained the situation to her and she cried with me. She explained that she and her husband also had young children at home and that this was their first trip away from them. I encouraged her to hug them extra hard when she got home.

That trip ended up being a tremendous blessing for us. It provided some space for us to process our grief on our own for a little bit before we were confronted by the sea of other people who were impacted by her death. No parent ever wants to have to make decisions about whether to have their child buried or cremated, but when those conversations must happen, they might as well take place in the most serene environment possible.

Fast forward to 2019. Kyle and I now had our son, Ryder, and we were pregnant with our daughter, Layne. We decided to take another trip to Mexico with some good friends who also had young children. One day we were out by the pool and someone in our group noticed another guest who appeared to be in a dour mood. "C'mon, dude, you're on vacation! What is there to be upset about in Mexico?" he joked. My eyes locked on Kyle's as I thought back to our trip in 2017. Even though our friend was just being lighthearted, it was a solid reminder that when we look at other people, we are only seeing a tiny fraction of the whole picture.

One of the many gifts that Ella has given us is the gift of empathy. After living through our experience, we are more likely than ever to cut people a generous amount of slack. Everybody has their own story beneath the surface, and we can all use a little extra grace. Even if someone isn't personally dealing with an awful situation, they may be supporting another person who is, and that is incredibly difficult as well.

THE RIPPLE EFFECT

When something terrible happens, it impacts you in unexpected ways, but it also impacts everyone around you. To this day, Kyle and I are still uncovering the rippling impact of our tragedy. When it happened, we were obviously at ground zero. It was all we could focus on, and everyone was tremendously supportive.

In retrospect, we have a clearer picture of the impact our loss had on others. Our parents not only lost a grandchild, but they also had to watch their own children go through unimaginable pain. Our siblings lost a niece, but most of them also had young children and were faced with the anxiety of knowing that something like this could happen to any of their kids. Many of our friends and neighbors have admitted to dealing with depression and anxiety following our tragedy.

It's easy to get caught up in what feels like a sucking black hole of grief, to be so consumed by what you lost that it's difficult to connect with those around you. I remember being reluctant to attend baby showers and birthday parties because I was afraid I might break down. I wanted to isolate myself from anything that would remind me of what I lost. The problem with isolation is that it causes you to lose touch with the fact that others are also grieving. Community is so important.

The more I took those steps forward to connect with others, the more I was able to experience the comfort that came from grieving together. Let's face it, there would be no way for me to protect myself from all the triggering painful things out there in the world. Instead, what I have learned to do is let them serve as reminders of how much I loved what I lost.

I have also allowed my heart to be softened to those around me. Everyone has their own worst thing, and we all deal with it differently. There is no way to accurately weigh one grief against another, so instead of feeling like my experience somehow opened this other dimension of grief that nobody can possibly understand, I'm just going to acknowledge that what I went through is awful. Also, other people are going through awful things, and I can be supportive of them.

STRUGGLING TO RELATE

One of the hardest, most isolating parts of grief is that often nobody knows what to say. This applies to both the griever and those trying to support them, but I've heard it most frequently from supporters. Kyle and I have joked around about writing a book on "What Not to Say to Grieving People." I think that book would sell, because people are terrified of saying the wrong thing. Conversely, some people need to read that book and don't even know it.

The whole situation is just funky. No words can make it better, but saying nothing feels wrong. When people try to fill that space with supportive sentiments, sometimes they say completely ridiculous and unhelpful things. Here was our approach as grievers— just be graceful to people.

Everyone is trying to be helpful, so sometimes you have to see the heart behind what they are saying, even if the words are totally wrong. People often try to relate based on what they have gone through, and if the worst pain they can think of is when they lost their dog, they may bring that up. Does that mean they think that losing a child is just like losing a dog? Probably not. They are just trying to empathize based on something that was very painful to them, so it doesn't make sense to get riled or try to set them straight.

Our stories are all different, and we all look at situations from our own frame of reference. When I met the woman by the pool in Mexico, she didn't cry with me because she missed Ella. She never even met Ella. She cried with me as a mother, thinking of her own children, and how painful it would be to move forward in this world without one of them.

People only have the capacity to relate based on what they have gone through. One beautiful aspect of our situation is that it has opened up a completely different frame of reference than we ever could have imagined. We are immediately safe people for anyone else to talk to about grief, because we get it on a very deep level. Even though this is not something we would have chosen, it is a tremendous silver lining.

COMPASSION HEALS

Part of what makes life meaningful is being able to enrich the lives of those around us. We wouldn't be able to do that if we were stuck in our own bitterness. Even more, the bitterness and anger wouldn't change anything. It would just make everyone around us miserable. Compassion is not only healing for others; I have found it to be like a salve for my own soul.

It is often said that hard times bring out the true nature of people. This applies to both the grievers and the supporters. In many ways, our tragedy revealed our true friends. It also repaired some broken friendships. There is something about the perspective that is gained through loss. It makes all the other nonimportant stuff just seem so petty.

At one point someone asked us, "What is the most surprising aspect of this whole experience?" For me, it was that we would one day be writing a book about it. I can't even begin to explain how helpless and lost I felt when Ella died. It would have completely blown my mind to think that one day I would be the one providing support to others in similar situations. During those initial moments at the hospital, all I wanted to do was wake from what felt like a nightmare. I wanted to run as far away as possible, but now here I am rushing back into those moments with others. It is really a mind-trip.

Our lives look so different now than we ever would have imagined, but part of what makes them so rich is our ability to help others. I read a quote from Rachel Marie Martin that said, "Sometimes you have to let go of the picture of what you thought your life would be like and learn to find joy in the story you are living" (Martin 2018). She's right. There is freedom in appreciating where we are in this story and the good that can come out of it. It doesn't make us any less sad about what we lost, but it does make it a little easier to move forward.

The Empty Pitcher

*A loss doesn't decrease your ability to love
other things, and having other things
doesn't diminish the loss.*

THE REPLACEMENT CHILD

Back when we were dating, Betty and I used to joke about how many children we would have. I would always say two, and she would tease me that I really meant three or four. We both knew that I meant two.

It hit me at some point right after our tragedy that we might actually have more than two children. Something about that felt very wrong to me. I had been so resolute that we would only have two kids. On the other hand, I wanted our next child to have a living sibling, which meant that I was now OK with having three. I struggled to reconcile this inconsistency in myself. All I could think of was that it felt like replacing Ella, which made me uncomfortable.

THE NEW PITCHER

Now that we have talked to a number of other people in similar situations, I see that this is a common concern for grieving parents.

Nobody wants to feel like they are replacing the child they lost. I don't think there is a way to completely make that fear go away, but I can tell you on the other side of having two more children that my perspective has changed.

In the weeks leading up to the birth of our son, Ryder, Betty shared with me that even though she was excited to meet the new baby, she was also a little scared. She said when she gave birth to Ella, it was like someone gave her a "mommy pitcher" that was full. When Ella died it felt like that pitcher was poured out and handed back to her, empty. She was afraid that having a new child would fill up her mommy pitcher again and somehow she would miss Ella less.

What ended up happening was very different. It reminded me of something my mom used to say about how your ability to love multiplies with each child. She said when my older brother was born, she couldn't imagine loving anything more than him, and then she had me. Apart from my being the greatest baby in the world, she was surprised at how her capacity to love was able to grow. She describes the same thing happening again with my younger brother, who wasn't even the greatest baby to be born—at best he ranked second or third, but I digress.

Our experience when we had Ryder was similar to what my mom described. In no way did he replace any of the love or sadness we had for Ella. It was like someone gave us a new pitcher that was full. Nothing could ever refill our empty Ella pitcher. We will always have it, and we will always miss her. However, missing Ella doesn't take away any of the joy or love we have for our son. Somehow there is a balance between these two extreme emotions.

LIFE AFTER LOSS

Loss changes things. People say "time heals all wounds," but try telling that to someone who has lost an appendage. Yes, wounds heal, but some wounds are life-altering. You have to learn how to live life in a completely different way. You're not going to get over it or forget about it. You may even have phantom pains, but it doesn't mean you can't live a full and happy life.

What it could mean is that living a fulfilling life might take a little more effort than it did before. In sports you often hear about how a team "overcomes adversity" and how mistakes and losses have helped prepare a team to become better. In life we grow through hardship, mistakes, and misfortune. As we all know, pain is frequently associated with gaining strength.

Just like in strength training, or any physical rehab, your body needs time to rebuild after the pain. You have to be intentional about giving yourself the space and support you need to recover. For us, we leaned heavily on friends and family as we were figuring out our new normal.

If you take nothing else away from this chapter, know this: a loss doesn't decrease your ability to have joy in your life or to love. Also, living a happy life does not in any way diminish the loss. There is a balance between letting go and remembering. Betty and I are still figuring it out every day. Even though it is true that wounds heal over time, it is also true that they leave scars, and some scars will always be tender.

THE TRUTH ABOUT BOOTSTRAPS

So what about pulling yourself up by your bootstraps? The phrase has been around for nearly two hundred years. It implies that with enough gumption, you can succeed without help from others. But it originated as an adage to describe an impossible task. If you were actually to grab the back of your boots or shoes and try to lift yourself up, you would probably be sitting on the floor right now.

Dealing with grief is like that. It isn't the type of thing you should attempt to figure out on your own. Your support system may look different from ours, but overcoming tragedy takes a village. It doesn't have to be a large village, but don't be afraid to phone a friend.

We talked a lot in the earlier chapters about focusing on the positives of what you have and appreciating the new perspective of the things you can't change. Positivity helps, but sometimes stuff happens in life that sucks, and no amount of focusing on silver linings makes it better. It's not just OK for you to be sad. It's expected. And asking for help isn't weak.

BITTERSWEET AVATAR

When we see other kids who were born around the same time as Ella, we often find ourselves realizing how old Ella would have been or saying, *Can you imagine having a five-year-old going to kindergarten right now?* Seeing the milestones of friends' and neighbors' kids as they continue to grow is a reminder of where Ella would have been in life. Sometimes these reminders are difficult, and sometimes they're life-affirming. Finding balance between avoiding things that trigger pain and keeping her memory alive is a must.

We believe an important part of this balance is the perspective we choose. For example, we saw pictures of some neighborhood girls, all Ella's age, having a tea party. I'm sure if Ella were around today, she would have been invited to the party. Those are the girls she would have grown up with and gone to school with. They are a reminder of where Ella would be in life. It would be easy to look at situations like this and let all the negative feelings rush back: bitterness, anger. Instead, we choose to separate these interactions from the loss and use them as a reminder that what we had was real.

We've done our best to avoid cutting out reminders and in some instances we've strengthened those relationships. When Ella was around three months old, she met her best friend and most direct avatar, Nora. We were going out for brunch (which is one of Betty's favorite activities) at *The Shack*. While waiting for a table we were sitting next to another couple with their own baby in a pumpkin seat. Nora was about six weeks older than Ella, so opening up with a conversation about the kids was natural. Being a few weeks older, Nora was hitting her milestones a bit ahead of Ella, and she gave us a pretty good idea of what was to come.

After Ella's passing, we didn't want to cut Nora or her parents, Andrew and Alison, out of our lives. Instead of pushing them away, our relationship has only gotten stronger. They have become some of our best friends. They've since moved to Michigan, but we make it a point to visit each other regularly or vacation together. Seeing the new milestones Nora hits continues to be a great reminder of where our own daughter would have been. It is bittersweet, but we choose to savor the sweet.

NEW DEPTH

Reflecting back on my multiple pitchers, I understand that my life has more depth now than ever before. I have experienced a loss so deep that I can better appreciate the fullness I have in other areas, even more profoundly. Carrying an empty pitcher is a reminder of what I had, and it is part of what gives me so much strength in moving forward.

Even when it is uncomfortable to lean on others, I have learned that it is worth it. I make it a point to avoid shutting myself off when support from others will be helpful. Also, I try to carry an awareness of those around me and offer support when I suspect they might be struggling.

Embracing the Contrast
Living Where the Darkness Meets the Light

AFTER THE TUNNEL

It has been said that "Grievers use a very simple calendar. Before and After." Life on the other side of the tunnel looks different. Grief is not something you ever get over—it changes you. We have been profoundly impacted by the death of our daughter. In truth, we are still in the process of learning what it looks like to live in this space where the darkness meets the light.

One thing we know is that the value Ella added to our lives far outweighs the pain of losing her. Having said that, nothing makes the pain completely go away. Some days are harder than others. Even though the tunnel is a helpful analogy, grief is not quite so linear. It is incredibly complex, and part of what has helped us move forward is being able to accept the messiness.

CHAPTER 8

Silver Linings

*It's about finding light in the darkness,
or sometimes even creating light.*

JOY AND PAIN

There is a strange connection between pain and joy. According to an article on Healthline.com, scientists have found that being tickled actually stimulates the same area of the brain that controls pain responses. This connection is why the movements of a person who is being tickled are so similar to those of someone in severe pain. In fact, tickling triggers both pain and touch nerve receptors (McDermott 2022).

A quick online search will provide loads of information about the connection between laughter and tears, but one particularly helpful insight for me came from the book *Laugh Your Way to Happiness: Use the Science of Laughter for Total Well-Being* by Lesley Lyle. Lyle explains that the psoas, which is the large muscle that draws the knees towards the hips and torso, is involved in our stress response. She says:

"The theory is that all mammals are genetically encoded so that this muscle is activated when the stress response is triggered, as this enables a creature to fight or flee. Afterward, the animal will shake or tremble in order to release the psoas, which clears tension and allows the autonomic nervous system to bring the body back into a state of relaxation" (Lyle 2014).

Lyle goes on to explain that humans have this same natural response to stress, but even though we tend to tremble as children, when we grow up we inhibit this response because it is seen as a sign of weakness. If you have ever seen anyone in a state of extreme emotional shock, or been in one yourself, you know that shaking is a very common response. Lyle points out a theory that we store unreleased trauma in contracted muscles. Well, the psoas is directly attached to the diaphragm, and you can imagine what happens when we laugh. Perhaps this explains why people often find themselves in tears after laughing for an extended period of time. There is something about laughter that is very emotionally balancing.

ELLA'S ARTWORK

Warning: This section provides details about our daughter's story, which could be triggering. Feel free to skip ahead to the next section.

I remember when Kyle and I had to go pick up Ella's belongings from the daycare. It was an incredibly difficult experience. Not only did all her belongings smell like her and carry special memories, but it was also a chance to connect with her caregivers. These are ladies who loved our daughter like their own. Needless to say, we knew when we pulled up to the building that we were in for an emotional exchange.

When we walked in the front door, the whole team of Ella's caregivers were waiting for us. Most of them had tears already streaming down their cheeks. We hugged each of them as they shared their condolences. It felt so surreal to be back in this place without her. The director of the daycare handed us her diaper bag and informed us that the team had prepared a gift.

A couple of workers brought out large packages wrapped in brown paper. When we unwrapped them, we were completely undone. They had taken two pieces of artwork that Ella had made in the week prior to her death and mounted them in beautiful golden frames. My heart broke as I traced the tiny fingerprints through the glass.

After many more hugs and tears, we went out to load our precious treasures into the car. As we pulled out of the parking lot to drive home, I broke down into gut-wrenching sobs. My face was a mess of snot and tears, and I will never forget what happened next.

Kyle gently placed his hand on my leg and said in the sweetest, most sincere voice, "To be fair, her artwork is probably worth much more now that she's gone." At once, I stopped crying and looked up at him. All of a sudden, I burst into uncontrollable laughter. I'm sure I seemed like a complete lunatic, but there was no judgment from Kyle, who laughed right along with me.

That moment in the car was exactly what it needed to be. It also perfectly illustrates this odd dissonance between pain and joy. Although they are opposite ends of the spectrum, they help to balance each other out. Even though laughter doesn't take the pain away, it allows you to come up for air. In an interview with the *Star Tribune*, Dr. Melissa Baartman Mork, a psychology professor and grief counselor, said, "Humor is more than being hilarious. It's facing our losses with optimism, gratitude, hope, even joy. It's the umbrella for approaching the tasks of grief with bravery and zest" (Burger 2019).

THE SILVER LININGS PAGE

If you were to ask what the single most helpful thing has been in our approach to grief, I would probably tell you the Silver Linings page in our journal. We knew when we started out on this journey that our natural tendency would be to focus on everything we lost, but on the third page of our journal, we started a very intentional list. We wanted to seek out and write down the positive things that have come about because of our tragedy.

What started as a few messy bullet points soon turned into a massive list. This is easily the most well-read portion of our journal. When sitting down and talking to other grieving people, we constantly find ourselves referencing this section. It almost feels like saying, "Hey, welcome to the club that nobody wants to be part of. It mostly sucks, but it does come with some benefits. Let us help illuminate a few of them for you." Here are some the highlights we often share:

- We have had a front row seat to see the goodness in other people. It doesn't make the pain easier, but it is still great to see what people are capable of in a broken world. Hard times truly bring out incredible kindness and generosity in others. Also, we discovered that we have an amazing support system that was beyond what we could have imagined before we fell into it and felt it flex around us.
- We have new relationships with amazing people we never would have met. We have made connections with other grieving parents who are spreading joy in the world in inspiring ways. We have formed connections with employees at St. Louis Children's Hospital, people who choose to expose themselves to difficult moments like the ones we have faced. We now have connections with incredibly generous business owners who have supported our fundraising efforts. We have a phenomenal network of publishing connections who have supported us in bringing this book to life, and we can't even begin to imagine all the amazing new people we will cross paths with as Ella's legacy continues to unfold.

- Our marriage is stronger than ever before. We've had to develop better communication as we were forced to work our way through the most difficult situation we could ever imagine. We now have a special bond that holds us together because nobody else understands what we have been through like each other does. Also, we were able to spend some very special time with each other in the months after we lost Ella, traveling and making memories before our next child was born.

- Everything else bad in life seems a little less awful when you have been through the worst-case scenario. Simple fears are easier to shrug off, like not being afraid of turbulence anymore. Also, when our car got stolen out of our garage, we weren't overwhelmed. The officers who came to the scene noted that we were surprisingly calm. I replied, "Oh, this isn't the worst thing that's ever happened to us."

- We have more courage now than ever before. For example, I never dreamed of getting a tattoo, but now I have one in Ella's memory. Also, we never dreamed of writing a book, but here we are. In general, we are willing to take more risks because we know life is short.

- We are better parents with our two other kids. We are more patient when they are being difficult. We take tons of pictures to capture every moment because we know that nobody is promised tomorrow. Our kids are the most valuable things in our lives, and we do our best to cherish even the little moments with them.

- We are more intentional about making the most of the time we have. We bought a cabin to renovate and create memories. We prioritize travel with our kids. Most importantly, we don't sweat the small stuff.

- Our sacrifice has created authority for us to speak and help others dealing with a loss and grief. We now have credibility and insight to share with other grieving people. We also have the ability to influence people who are supporting those who are grieving.

- We're more patient and have more empathy for others. Our frame of reference now includes deep tragedy that allows us to better relate to others. We are more likely to give people the benefit of the doubt because we know what it is like to have a huge iceberg beneath the surface.

- The lower lows we've experienced have helped to create higher highs in life. The contrast of darkness creates brights that are even more brilliant. Similar to looking up at the stars in a dark field, contrast is necessary to accentuate the dark and light. After losing Ella, our experience of having Ryder was somehow enhanced beyond explanation.

- We get to see and participate in our daughter's legacy. Most parents only hope their children will change the world— we know Ella did. She inspires us every day to impact the world in a positive way.

HOPE IS NOT A PLAN

Back when Kyle and I first met in a project management class as part of our MBA program, we had a professor who would often say, "Hope is not a plan." We frequently tease each other with this phrase, but one day as we were journaling, Kyle turned it around. He said, "You know, I'm realizing that even though 'hope is not a plan,' sometimes having a plan can give you hope."

Thinking back to the early days of our tragedy, I remember feeling like so much was outside of our control. Everyone around us was eager to help, but it felt like we were just floating, and all these helpful resources just seemed to be bobbing in the water around us. It wasn't until we moved from floating to swimming that things started to get better. We were able to find a positive way to channel our energy and gather up some of the monetary gifts that were given for a good cause.

I remember the day we walked into St. Louis Children's hospital with a check to set up Ella's endowment fund. So many memories hit me when we came through the front door. Our last visit there had been filled with feelings of chaos and helplessness. This time was very different. We were there with purpose, and we had a plan to make things better.

We had tossed around a number of ideas of what we could do with the money people had donated to us in Ella's memory. We considered making improvements at the hospital or purchasing additional resources to help make heart families more comfortable during their time there, but in the end we decided our true passion was in keeping them from having to be there in the first place.

Even though we realized we would likely never see a direct outcome, we decided to designate the funds toward pediatric heart research. We knew that nothing could bring our daughter back, but the thought of keeping something like this from happening to another family gave us hope. Through various fundraising activities, like a trivia night we hold every year around Ella's birthday, and other personal donations, the Ella Marie Endowment Fund has now accumulated over $58,000.

In 2020 we learned that Kory Lavine, MD, PhD, a cardiologist and researcher at the Children's Discovery Institute, had applied for a research grant from the fund. His ultimate goal was to learn why heart failure develops and how best to treat it individually based on each person's unique genetics. Dr. Lavine shared that "more than 40 percent of patients with dilated cardiomyopathy [Ella's cause of death] have identifiable genetic mutations that affect how the heart muscle contracts. Each mutation ultimately points to a specific, individual reason for heart failure" (St. Louis Children's Hospital, 2019).

According to Dr. Lavine, "Kids have the biggest need to identify diagnostic and therapeutic approaches to treat the cause of their heart failure." Because standard heart failure medications for adults aren't effective in children, he and his research team are collaborating to identify drugs that will target those mutations for heart failure, specifically in pediatric patients. Not only is this amazing work being funded in Ella's name, but we found out that they are actually using donated tissue from her heart in their research.

STRENGTH WE WOULDN'T CHOOSE

People often say, "I could never go through what you've been through," but it's surprising what you are capable of when you don't have a choice. Pain is often involved in gaining strength. Sometimes we choose to push ourselves to get stronger, and sometimes painful things just happen and strength is the result.

When we first lost Ella, it felt like someone took our most precious possession and just poured it down the drain. Her life felt completely wasted. Now I realize that is not the case. We are getting a front row seat to her incredible legacy, and our other two kids are really going to have to be world-changers to live up to the high standard their sister set for them.

Our lives are not ruined because we lost Ella. They are enriched because we had her. She made us stronger, better versions of ourselves. Her story is not a dark cloud that has cast an ominous shadow on the rest of our lives. She is the source of more silver linings than we will ever even know.

Living Where the Darkness Meets the Light

If we can live through this, we can do anything.

THE EPIC COMEBACK

Every compelling plot line contains adversity. The contrast of the hero's struggle throughout the story makes the end victory even more powerful. The movie *Rudy* does a great job at delivering on this tension. Rudy has a dream to play football at Notre Dame. He doesn't have money for tuition nor the grades for a scholarship. He struggles even to get accepted into the school. He goes to try-outs as a "walk-on," knowing that it is a long shot for him to make the team. He ends up making the practice squad because of his work ethic, and after a year of supporting everyone else with no payoff, he finally gets to dress for one game—the last game of his senior year.

In an awe-inspiring moment, Rudy leads the team onto the field. He spends the entire game on the sidelines until the final drive. With the game all but wrapped up, every senior player, except Rudy, is sent onto the field. The crowd begins to chant his name, "Rudy, Rudy . . ." until the sound fills the stadium. Finally, the head coach gives Rudy a chance to get on the field. On the final play of the game, Rudy sacks the quarterback and is carried out on the shoulders of his teammates in front of a roaring crowd. The movie notes that no other player had ever been carried off the same way. The contrast of where Rudy started to where he ended up is what makes this moment so epic.

Sports in general are full of highs and lows. Kyle has been a fan of the St. Louis Blues since he can remember. They have had good teams in the past, but never good enough to make it all the way to a championship. Although the Blues made it to the Stanley Cup finals their first three years in the league, they got swept every time. For the next fifty years, they never made it back.

After all the years of disappointment, it was hard to stay optimistic, even as a loyal fan. When they made the championship run again in 2019, it was electric. Overcoming all the odds, they came from last place in the league to finally win the Stanley Cup. The whole journey was an incredible experience that Kyle will never forget. Somehow the previous years of disappointments had made their victory even more powerful.

Just like in these examples, your tragedy has set you up for an epic comeback. Similar to Rudy and the St. Louis Blues, you have come face to face with the heaviness of loss and defeat. However, that loss is not the end of your story.

POST-TRAUMATIC GROWTH

In his book *Flourish*, Martin E.P. Seligman talks about the concept of post-traumatic growth (PTG) within the context of military training. He shares that even though "a substantial number of people show intense depression and anxiety after extreme adversity . . . then they grow. In the long run, they arrive at a higher level of psychological functioning than before" (Seligman 2011). This is not anecdotal. It is a statement of fact.

Seligman talks about a study that was conducted based on a questionnaire that listed fifteen of the worst things that can happen to a person in life: torture, death of a child, rape, terminal illness, and so on. Over the course of one month, seventeen hundred individuals reported at least one of these terrible events and then took the well-being test. The findings were clear that people who had experienced more trauma were actually stronger and had higher well-being scores than their counterparts. Seligman describes trauma as a fork in the road that "enhances the appreciation of paradox. Loss and gain both happen. Grief and gratitude both happen. Vulnerability and strength both happen." He goes on to clarify that "this is not remotely to suggest that we celebrate trauma itself; rather that we should make the most of the fact that the trauma often sets the stage for growth" (Seligman 2011).

FINDING YOUR FIRE

The stage has been set, and you get to choose what comes next. This is the best part. There are endless possibilities for your story. You just have to think about what you want your journey to look like. We have been incredibly inspired by some other couples who have experienced similar tragedies to ours, so we wanted to share a couple of their stories with you.

OLLIE'S STORY

Our first exposure to the Ollie Hinkle Heart Foundation was when we were in the hospital with Ella. She was at a developmental stage in which all she wanted to do was crawl around and put everything in her mouth, which made it very difficult to live in a hospital room. One of the nurses offered to bring in some large mats to put on the floor so Ella could play, and we noticed that they had an Ollie Hinkle Heart Foundation logo on them.

The mission of the Ollie Hinkle Heart Foundation is to strengthen and empower families affected by congenital heart disease. It was built on the love Mark and Jenn Hinkle were shown after their son Ollie passed away from a congenital heart defect (CHD) at age one. Jenn shares about her experience,

"I fell to the ground. I didn't have the strength to stand up, and a cry came out of me that I'd never heard before. My husband and my father-in-law picked me up off the floor—literally and figuratively—they held me up and surrounded me with their love. And soon family and friends came from near and far and wrapped our family in love. Then acquaintances. Then complete strangers. And the circle surrounding us grew and grew. Through all that we received, we found peace, hope, and strength to keep going. And eight years later, that continues to grow as we SPREAD LOVE to others through the Foundation we began in his name. It is thanks to all of that love and support that the OHHF has positioned itself as one of the leading resources for heart families in St. Louis and beyond." (OHHF 2021)

The foundation wraps families in love, provides medical and mental health support, and funds impactful and innovative technology (OHHF 2021). Jenn and Mark have played an important role in our story, and countless other families' stories, all because they took their tragedy and turned it into something beautiful. What better way to honor their son?

JACKSON'S STORY

We crossed paths with Lara and Ben Gillham after being introduced through a mutual acquaintance. We quickly discovered that our stories were remarkably similar. Their six-month-old son, Jackson Gillham, had been admitted to the hospital with what appeared to be cold symptoms but turned out to be a much more serious condition. A CT scan revealed that Jackson had a rare heart defect that took his life before he was able to have surgery.

The Gillhams were absolutely crushed by their tragedy and had trouble finding other people who could relate to them. After identifying the gap in support, they decided to become part of the solution. They partnered with another couple, Martha and Nick McGeehon, who had unexpectedly lost their healthy four-month-old daughter, Everly, a few months before Jackson died. Together they created a nonprofit called Just Enduring: Living & Loving After Child Loss.

The purpose of Just Enduring is to provide support for families in the earliest days of grief. The two couples, along with the help of Dr. Ken Remy, a critical care physician, and his wife, Allison Remy, a palliative care social worker, are now delivering on this mission. They have launched a website with resources and stories to help grieving parents and tips for family and friends wanting to support bereaved loved ones. They have also set up a mentoring program to connect parents who have experienced similar losses so they can support each other.

Instead of allowing their experiences to make them isolated and bitter, they created an amazing support network in honor of their children. They knew that these conversations with other parents would likely bring up very raw and painful emotions for them, but still they pressed on. Their decision to engage will impact countless lives moving forward. What an incredible legacy for Jackson and Everly.

ACTS OF KINDNESS

Making a difference can happen on any scale. You don't have to go out and start a nonprofit. Sometimes healing can come from helping others in small ways. We have been teaching our children to celebrate their sister's legacy through random acts of kindness, a very hands-on approach for keeping Ella's memory alive.

For example, we painted kindness rocks to leave at a local park to make other people smile. Randomly, we send cards and drawings to people to tell them how much we love and appreciate them. We take special trips in Ella's honor to build memories for our family. We surprise people with unexpected gifts. We are always thinking of new ways to make the world a brighter place because of Ella.

The possibilities are endless and inspiration is everywhere. It is all part of finding this new way to live in which the brokenness can walk hand-in-hand with hope. Our loss of Ella doesn't have to stay buried in some dark corner in the past. Her memories can coexist with beautiful, joy-filled moments in the present and the future.

Her role in our family is just as important now as it ever was, and that will never change. Our lives have more beauty and depth because we had Ella. She made us stronger, broadened our perspective, introduced us to new friends, opened doors for us to help others, and taught us never to take a day for granted.

THE ROAD AHEAD

So here we are at the end of our time together. We have done our best to share with you some insights that have been helpful to us, but our journey is far from over. For the rest of our lives we will be in the process of figuring out what it looks like to live where the darkness meets the light. Our goal in writing this book was simply to walk along beside you and provide some encouragement for the road ahead.

We hope some of the notes from our journal have been helpful to you. As a quick recap: We started by acknowledging that there can be beauty in every situation. We shared about how wrong turns can provide us with a fresh perspective. We talked about how life is short and comparison is flawed. We wrestled with negative emotions and acknowledged how important it is to communicate. We decided that instead of being hardened by our tragedy, we would allow it to make us even more empathetic and compassionate to those around us. We realized that our loss does not take away our capacity for joy, and that joy will never diminish our sadness. And lastly, we recognized that our lives have not been ruined by what we lost, but they are deeper and richer because of what we had.

Brené Brown once said, "One day you will tell your story of how you overcame what you went through and it will be someone else's survival guide" (Brown 2021). Now you've heard our story. It's time for you to write your own. If we could leave you with one recommendation, it would be an encouragement to journal. Not only was the journaling process helpful for us to unravel our thoughts and connect with each other, but we now have it to look back on and remember what we learned.

Right after we lost Ella, all we wanted to do was run away from the pain. Journaling about it was not easy. Now that we look back, we are so glad we documented some of those moments. As painful as it was at the time, the farther we get away from the situation, the fuzzier those memories become. We are very grateful to have a record.

Like us, you probably have more exposure now than you ever wanted to have to the topic of grief. You are now part of the tribe of unlikely experts. Be prepared, because down the road others may come to you and ask for your insight. You are now in a unique position to walk with people during these heavy moments. We hope you find it as rewarding as we have found this opportunity to walk with you.

GOLDEN THREADS

We want to leave you with something that has really resonated with us. In Japan, there is an art form called kintsugi. The word kintsugi literally translates to "golden joinery." This ancestral art form takes broken pottery and repairs it with gold. It celebrates the idea that there is tremendous beauty in the broken. Instead of hiding the cracks, the gold highlights them as a focal point. The result is a stunning new piece of artwork that is even more valuable than before it was damaged.

Our tragedy was crushing, but it did not destroy us. When we look at our lives now, we see cracks, but we will continue to mend them with gold. Morgan Harper Nichols says it beautifully: "May you never forget how far you have come, for you have traveled many miles to get to this place. May you never forget the starless nights that shaped you and the morning skies that gave you the hope and strength to carry on. For after all the years you have made it through, over and over, light has found its way to you and even though you still have a long way to go, all the miles you have traveled matter more than you know" (Nichols 2018).

These are our hopes for you: that you are able to embrace your imperfect path, and grow to have a richer, deeper life than you ever could have imagined. When you look at all the miles you've traveled, may you never forget the brokenness that has given you strength. And perhaps above all, we hope you may truly be able to appreciate the beauty in the threads of gold that hold all the pieces together.

Acknowledgments

Just as we worked to capture silver linings in our journal, we also want to take the time to document the village of people it took to bring this book to life. They have been our shining stars throughout this project, providing us with enough light to take our next steps. When we set out on this journey, we had absolutely no idea what an undertaking it would be. We owe a huge debt of gratitude to the following people:

A very special thanks to both our families for all the countless hours you put into reading drafts, brainstorming titles/taglines, providing design feedback, listening to us talk about progress, and believing in us to complete what we set out to do.

A specific thank you to Pam Kraus, who championed us throughout the entire process, encouraging us when we felt disheartened, helping us find the words when we were struggling, and never letting us forget why we started.

Another specific thanks to Lynn Mertens, who was always such a strong sounding board, providing valuable insights and perspective, along with beautifully crafting our logo.

To all our friends and endorsers who took the time to read our manuscript and provide us with thoughtful and honest feedback.

To our dear friend Bree Friedrichs, who is uniquely gifted at wrapping words around messy moments, and who offered us the type of support and companionship we hope to provide to others.

To Julie Winkle Giulioni, who believed in us and connected us with an amazingly talented tribe of people in the publishing industry who are phenomenal at their jobs.

To Anne Janzer, who painstakingly answered all our questions and gently guided us through the writing process.

To Paul Wright, whose brilliant mind helped sharpen our work in ways beyond what we could have contrived on our own.

To Becky Robinson, who taught and inspired us to reach more readers than we ever could have thought possible.

To Nikki Soulsby, who served as both a mentor and friend on the writing journey.

To Dan Wright, who tirelessly encouraged us to keep writing and never stopped cheering for us along the way.

To Julie Haase, who is incredibly talented at her job and an absolute joy to work with.

To Carla Green, the most knowledgeable, patient, and gracious book designer of all time.

To Ben and Lara Gillham, for helping us build a website and establish a nonprofit when we had no idea what we were doing.

To Chelsea Vaughn, for designing a beautiful logo for Ella's Umbrella.

To Anna Archibald, for watching our kids so we could write.

To Erin Hodges, for capturing beautiful author photos for our book cover and website.

And most of all, to Ella for inspiring us to leave this world a better place than we found it.

Bibliography

Begley, Sharon. 2007. *Train Your Mind, Change Your Brain: How a New Science Reveals Our Extraordinary Potential to Transform Ourselves*. New York: Ballantine Books.

Burger, Kevyn. 2019. "Working through grief? A 'certified humor professional' is here to help." Startribune.com. Accessed November 4, 2021. https://www.startribune.com/working-through-grief-a-certified-humor-professional-is-here-to-help/558574732/.

Brown, Brené. 2015. *Daring Greatly: How the Courage to Be Vulnerable Transforms the Way We Live, Love, Parent, and Lead*. New York: Avery.

Brown, Brené. 2021. Accessed January 9, 2022. Insightoftheday.com. https://www.insightoftheday.com/motivational-quote-by-brene-brown-05-06-2021.

Dolan, Paul. 2014. *Happiness by Design: Change What You Do, Not How You Think*. New York: Hudson Street Press.

Ferriss, Timothy. 2017. *Tribe of Mentors: Short Life Advice from the Best in the World*. Boston: Houghton Mifflin Harcourt.

Hawthorne, Jennifer. 2014. "Change Your Thoughts, Change Your World." jenniferhawthorne.com. Accessed August 3, 2019. http://www.jenniferhawthorne.com/articles/change_your_thoughts.html.

Herbert, Frank. 2019. *Dune*. New York: Ace.

Kogan, Nataly. 2018. *Happier Now: How to Stop Chasing Perfection and Embrace Everyday Moments (Even the Difficult Ones)*. Boulder: Sounds True.

Kwapis, Ken, dir. 2013. *The Office*. Season 9, episode 23. "Finale." Aired May 16, 2013, on NBC.

Lesser, Casey. 2018. "The Centuries-Old Japanese Tradition of Mending Broken Ceramics with Gold." Artsy. Accessed November 9, 2021. https://www.artsy.net/article/artsy-editorial-centuries-old-japanese-tradition-mending-broken-ceramics-gold.

Lyle, Lesley. 2014. *Laugh Your Way to Happiness: Use the Science of Laughter for Total Well-Being*. London: Watkins Publishing.

Martin, Rachel Marie. 2018. *The Brave Art of Motherhood: Fight Fear, Gain Confidence, and Find Yourself Again*. Colorado Springs: WaterBrook.

McDermott, Annette. 2022. "Why Are People Ticklish?" Healthline. Accessed December 4, 2021. https://www.healthline.com/health/why-are-people-ticklish.

McInerny, Nora. 2019. *We Don't "Move On" from Grief. We Move Forward with It*. Posted April 25, 2019. TED video, 15:06. https://www.youtube.com/watch?v=khkJkR-ipfw.

Nichols, Morgan Harper. 2018. Instagram. Accessed January 9, 2022. https://www.instagram.com/p/BeJcoXrDFG7/.

Nunez, Paul L. 2016. *The New Science of Consciousness: Exploring the Complexity of Brain, Mind, and Self*. Amherst, NY: Prometheus Books.

OHHF (Ollie Hinkle Heart Foundation). n.d. About page. Accessed December 3, 2021. https://www.theohhf.org/about/.

Richman, Linda. 2001. *I'd Rather Laugh: How to Be Happy Even When Life Has Other Plans for You*. New York: Warner Books.

Sandberg, Sheryl, & Grant, Adam. 2017. *Option B: Facing Adversity, Building Resilience, and Finding Joy*. New York: Alfred A. Knopf.

Seligman, Martin E.P. 2011. *Flourish: A Visionary New Understanding of Happiness and Well-Being.* New York: Free Press.

St. Louis Children's Hospital. 2019. "A Brighter Future for Children with Genetic Heart Defects." Great News Newsletter. Printed by St. Louis Children's Hospital.

van der Kolk, Bessel A. 2015. *The Body Keeps the Score: Brain, Mind, and Body in the Healing of Trauma.* New York: Penguin Books.

Weekes, Claire. 1995. *Self-Help for Your Nerves: Learn to Relax and Enjoy Life Again by Overcoming Stress and Fear.* United Kingdom: HarperCollins Publishers.

About the Authors

Kyle and Betty Mertens were inspired to become authors after the tragic loss of their daughter Ella. In an effort to keep their grief from pulling them apart, they leaned into one another and created a shared journal. Through their notes, they ended up uncovering principles that not only strengthened their marriage but also proved helpful to others who had experienced loss.

Kyle and Betty have now taken those insights and written them into a book. Their mission is to provide support for grieving people and those around them during difficult times when nobody knows what to say. Using stories and humor to take some of the weight off of heavy moments, they partner with the reader like a close friend and walk along beside them on the journey.

*A portion of the proceeds from this book will go to **Ella's Umbrella**, a nonprofit that funds pediatric cardiology research, supports cardiac technology advancements, and provides encouragement for people facing unimaginable circumstances.*

A Note from the Authors

It has been an honor and a privilege to join you on this journey. We have no idea what caused you to pick up this book, but our deepest hope is that it was encouraging to you. If we knew your name, we would add it to the silver linings page of our journal.

We want to continue to be a resource for you, so please look us up online at **www.kyleandbetty.com** or email us at **kyleandbetty mertens@gmail.com**.

If our book was helpful, we hope you will consider recommending it to others. We would also appreciate any reviews on Amazon. This is a great way to help other folks find our book and give us meaningful feedback on how we can better support people in the future.

www.ingramcontent.com/pod-product-compliance
Lightning Source LLC
Chambersburg PA
CBHW020424130626
46549CB00006B/2728